PRAISE FOR *THE WOLVES AND THE MANDOLIN*

"*What an extraordinary true story of courage, tenacity, focus, and perseverance . . . and sometimes the intervention of fate. Brandon Vallorani chronicles the courageous and perilous journey of his great-grandfather, Papa Luigi. I highly recommend every entrepreneur and business owner read his story and study the valuable leadership lessons it reveals. When life's problems seem overwhelming, you'll think of Papa Luigi and realize the wolf at your door isn't all that scary.*"

—LUCY HOGER, CEO and Growth Strategist,
Visionocity

"*Brandon Vallorani is a risk taker, and risk takers built America. He seizes opportunity the way Julius Caesar seized ancient citadels. Brandon has one of the greatest marketing minds at work today. Everyone that dreams of building a great business should stop and listen carefully to the advice Brandon Vallorani gives in his book* The Wolves and the Mandolin. *Advice this good demands your attention.*"

—FLOYD BROWN, CEO,
USA Radio Networks

"Luigi's pursuit of the American Dream still lives within his great-grandson. Much as Luigi stood his ground during battles in Benghazi and Sciara, Brandon's perseverance and old-world determination has enabled him to maintain his entrepreneurial spirit and succeed while dodging his own bullets in the form of two recessions. This journey is as much about a family's history as it is our nation's."

—STEVEN A. CASTLETON, recipient,
US Army Outstanding Civilian Service Medal

"My mother told me to never run with the herd because it is usually going the wrong way. Brandon Vallorani's ambitious book, The Wolves and the Mandolin, is a reminder that if your goals are big enough and you are audacious enough, you will find the strength to keep persisting until you succeed. You can live the life that God intended for you to live."

—STEVEN F. HOTZE, MD, founder and CEO,
Hotze Health & Wellness Center

"Brandon Vallorani's The Wolves and the Mandolin is a mellifluous blend of life and business lessons wrapped up in the actions and approaches taken by his Italian ancestors from a bygone era. Prepare to be educated, inspired, and entertained simultaneously. Bravo, Brandon!"

—MONICA LUEDECKE, President,
Hotze Enterprises

"*Brandon Vallorani takes us on a 'Godfather-esque' journey through his ancestors' lives and how the lessons they've learned still apply to our everyday lives today. He quickly integrates you into the picturesque, brutal, and sobering world of good versus evil and family pride. With a humble appreciation for his past, Vallorani reveals his ancestors' sacrifices and how much their decisions impacted his very existence. Having had an uncle who stood on the deck of a warship engaging the enemy during the attack of Pearl Harbor, I'm grateful to Brandon for telling his story. Don't miss this book chock-full of amazing stories and life lessons!*"

—SCOT FERRELL, national and international best-selling author (*It's Not Them, It's You*), speaker, and media personality; behavior coach and consultant to CEOs and executives; Founder and President, The Scot Ferrell Companies

The WOLVES and the MANDOLIN

The
W🐺LVES
and the
MAND🎻LIN

CELEBRATING LIFE'S PRIVILEGES IN A HARSH WORLD

BRANDON VALLORANI

ForbesBooks

Published by ForbesBooks, Charleston, South Carolina.
Member of Advantage Media Group.

ForbesBooks is a registered trademark, and the ForbesBooks colophon is a trademark of Forbes Media, LLC.

Printed in the United States of America.

ISBN: 9780998365572
LCCN: 2017932189

Cover design by George Stevens.

This publication is designed to provide accurate and authoritative information in regard to the subject matter covered. It is sold with the understanding that the publisher is not engaged in rendering legal, accounting, or other professional services. If legal advice or other expert assistance is required, the services of a competent professional person should be sought.

Advantage Media Group is proud to be a part of the Tree Neutral® program. Tree Neutral offsets the number of trees consumed in the production and printing of this book by taking proactive steps such as planting trees in direct proportion to the number of trees used to print books. To learn more about Tree Neutral, please visit **www.treeneutral.com.**

Since 1917, the Forbes mission has remained constant. Global Champions of Entrepreneurial Capitalism. ForbesBooks exists to further that aim by bringing the Stories, Passion, and Knowledge of top thought leaders to the forefront. ForbesBooks brings you The Best in Business. To be considered for publication, please visit **www.forbesbooks.com.**

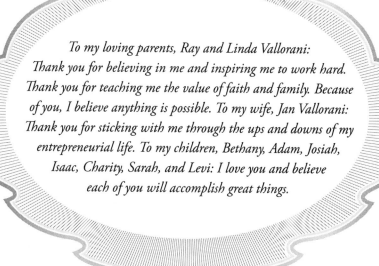

To my loving parents, Ray and Linda Vallorani:
Thank you for believing in me and inspiring me to work hard.
Thank you for teaching me the value of faith and family. Because
of you, I believe anything is possible. To my wife, Jan Vallorani:
Thank you for sticking with me through the ups and downs of my
entrepreneurial life. To my children, Bethany, Adam, Josiah,
Isaac, Charity, Sarah, and Levi: I love you and believe
each of you will accomplish great things.

TABLE OF CONTENTS

FOREWORD

"LEAVE THE GUN. TAKE THE CANNOLI."

S o quipped the fictional Italian America hitman Pete
Clemenza in a notable postassassination sequence famously
depicted in Francis Ford Coppola's cinematic adaptation
of Mario Puzo's *The Godfather*. Is this just some Hollywood ploy
inserted for levity after a brutal murder? Or is there something
deeper and necessary happening in this assassin's admittedly bent—
but still human—heart? Should one's work and life take the time to
include small enjoyments . . . like cannoli?

Brandon Vallorani masterfully demonstrates that despite the
inevitable presence of formidable wolves (and our own bent hearts),
there must be intentional times devoted to cultivating joy in small
things—that hard, entrepreneurial work on the one hand, with
enjoying good wine, fine cigars, and family on the other hand need
not be fierce competitors.

As a man of faith, Vallorani recognizes that life is not just *eternal*
but also must be *abundant* right now. It's certainly an Italian thing,
but really it should also be a human thing stemming from how we
were designed, thus it is an indispensable thing. But how? And why
does this fuel the spirit of the entrepreneur?

The Italian American story Vallorani weaves serves as the platform for pursuing, cultivating, and enjoying this abundant life, including the sustained full life of the entrepreneur. To understand Vallorani only by his marked success and heaving company revenues is to miss the ethos of why he's been successful. It's to confuse means with ends. And it's to miss being fully human.

What we see as Vallorani unfolds his jubilant entrepreneurial journey is that relationships trump transactions; flourishing motivates far more than fear; community prevails over commodity; and incarnation (living it) precedes proclamation (talking about it). And taking the time for good wine, fine cigars, and *la familia* fuels and sustains this abundant life. I know; I too come from a similar Italian American immigration narrative.

Vallorani's story and his keen practical insights offered in *The Wolves and the Mandolin* reflect an arc and pattern we must all increasingly emulate. He doesn't give us yet another recycled, mind-numbing checklist or yet another artificial, rote "how-to" formula but rather he causes us to focus on a higher, more human conception of the business vocation. He calls us to go well beyond making a living and instead challenges us to make a difference. The key is cultivating joy in small things, the human things, despite the reality of wolves. Vallorani's work, steeped in both respectful tradition and out-of-the-box innovation, exudes a contagious mind-set, posture, and vision for incubating and sustaining success. And yet, there's plenty of practical stuff here, too.

Vallorani demonstrates what success "looks like" in whatever endeavor, personal or professional. The successful person, the real and realistic person, will overcome the yapping and sometimes biting wolves by enjoying sweet respites with the mandolin. To understand this juxtaposition of wolf and mandolin, keep reading.

What is the pattern for sustained and rejuvenating success? Vallorani in essence shows us that we must recognize the following:

1. The successful person *inherits*. What do we have to learn from the past? There are valuable lessons to be inherited if we take the time to learn them, and Vallorani's Italian ancestors and their stories embody this truth.

2. The successful person *incarnates*. We may not simply know, but we must be and live what we know in order to be fully human—including taking the time and space to enjoy and rejuvenate around the small things.

3. The successful person *invests*. We are duty-bound to blessedly give, to enhance and promote the flourishing of others. Otherwise, our joy will be truncated and self-absorbedly crabbed—a lose/lose proposition, antithetical to the true entrepreneur.

Brandon Vallorani's journey and evident success—whether involving vineyards, cigars, or family—distills down to his fervent conviction rightly answering and ordering two key questions:

1. What can mankind *do*?
2. What is mankind *for*?

Only by first understanding the latter question can one rightly direct entrepreneurial energies toward the former for maximal flourishing and enjoyment so vital to a sustained abundant life, a life certainly lived among wolves but not defined by the wolves.

Rather, to expand the titular metaphor, a well-ordered, well-lived life features a soundtrack not dominated with rancorous howling and the baring of wolves' teeth; it's a soundtrack provided by a sweet melodious mandolin, a soundtrack of goodness, truth, and beauty best shared in relationships and moments with others generationally for their enjoyment, flourishing, and beauty.

Vallorani also understands that the world is a wheat field, not a weed field—he realistically calls us to deal with the weeds but not to dwell on them. No Pollyanna pabulum here.

Vision requires us to cultivate wheat and enjoy its harvest with others. As Augustine, who would have been an Italian if he had had a choice, counseled: "Love God, and do what you want." Rightly understood, this encapsulates the entrepreneur's mode. Vallorani models this humbly, but confidently, and calls us to this abundant life as well, loving God and almost recklessly doing what we want. Why? For the bigger things: we cannot "do good" unless we do things well, and enjoying the small things catalyzes doing things well.

Vallorani's story is thus one of sustaining a winning rhythm: ebb and flow, desire and design, leadership and learning, faith and fidelity, and loving, not merely tolerating, leisure such as actively resting in the abundant life with good wine, which makes the heart glad; with fine cigars, which are units of protected time, as another Italian friend quipped; with family because as Don Vito Corleone, also of *The Godfather*, warned, "A man who doesn't spend time with his family can never be a real man."

Brandon Vallorani is not a fictional man; Brandon, *my paisano* (pal), is a real man, and he knows what it takes to become and be a real man—and he shows us here that in that pursuit, one must enjoy the small things: good wine, a fine cigar, great coffee, *la familia*. And now he invites us into his story to promote the flourishing of others—a story best shared with others—to ponder, reflect, and enjoy the little things which propel us to the big things, the entrepreneurial things, and the permanent things . . . and it helps to do so with good wine, a fine cigar, and *la familia*. Can you hear the mandolin in the background? Turn up the volume, fill my glass, and pass the lighter. It's time to read.

JEFFERY J. VENTRELLA, J.D., PH.D.

SENIOR COUNSEL, SENIOR VICE PRESIDENT OF TRAINING

ALLIANCE DEFENDING FREEDOM

ACKNOWLEDGMENTS

Thank you, Dr. Steven Hotze, for inspiring me to write this book. Thank you, Liz Darnell, for your tireless assistance as I wrote this book. You have been my right arm for over ten years. Thank you, Gary DeMar, for giving me your blessing to start my own company while I was still working for you. Thank you, Jared Vallorani, for helping me lead Liberty Alliance as our CEO and achieve ranking on the *Inc.* 5000 list five years in a row. Thank you, Tracey Clarkson, for keeping up with me and for providing the financial leadership as my CFO that I needed over the years.

I owe a big thank you to Alison, Jenny, Helen, George, Katie, Shelby, and the rest of the team of editors, designers, and publicity gurus who work with Adam Witty at ForbesBooks. You helped make this book not just a goal but a reality. Thank you!

Last, heartfelt appreciation is due to the many who have been a part of my life over the years, though I may not have been able to mention each one of you by name. I wouldn't be who I am without your influence.

INTRODUCTION

THE WOLVES AND THE MANDOLIN— WHY THIS BOOK?

The future starts today, not tomorrow.

POPE JOHN PAUL II

T he legends we memorialize reflect a view of our place in this world and what it will be for generations who follow us. This is one story that has been passed down in my family.

The Wolves and the Mandolin

Deep in the rocky foothills of the Apennine Mountains of Abruzzo, Italy, lived a great-uncle who was a popular mandolin player. He would travel on foot far and wide to neighboring villages to play at a wedding or a festa and then walk the long miles back to his own village when the party was over.

These mountains were full of wolves, and the way was dark and lonely. One night, as he trudged the stony path back to his village from a party, he heard the unmistakable sounds of a pack of wolves gathering around him and quickly getting closer. You can imagine the prickles on the back of his neck as his eyes strained to locate shelter or a hiding place, but all he could see was one lone tree. It was better than nothing.

He scrambled up into its branches and managed to reach a crook at the top, just out of reach of the wolves. Knowing he would be forced to stay there until daybreak, he settled himself as best he could in his precarious perch.

The wolves gathered beneath him, jumping at the tree trunk, snapping their massive jaws at him. To while away the time, he began to play his beloved mandolin.

The sweet strains of beauty filled the darkness. His heartbeat calmed and his breath slowed, with the starry sky's expanse over him and the still night air clearing his lungs. Ahhh. What a privilege it is to be alive, he thought. But it is more than that. To be able to play beautiful music, to hear it, to breathe in the night air is a precious privilege indeed.

Soon, the baying and the snarling ceased. The wolves stopped stalking around the base of the tree. Calmed by the simple melodies he had played all night, my great-uncle found the wolves had stolen away before dawn, no longer a threat. He climbed down and continued home with quite a story to tell.

It's a classic story that my kids beg me to tell them over and over. But it's more than an exciting kid's tale of scary wolves growling with sharp teeth waiting to rip the man limb from limb. This tale speaks to the ideals of resilience, of staying calm under pressure, of dealing with danger and hardships in a smart and resolute way. This tale reminds us that beauty can be found even in the midst of growling wolves and that even the fiercest wolves can be calmed. This story reminds us to take the time to enjoy life's privileges in spite of the wolves we might face.

In my own visits to the Apennine foothills over the past decade, I have been struck by the beautiful landscape. This part of Italy hasn't been overrun by tourists and caterwauling vendors peddling selfie sticks and bottled water. It's the old Italy. Towns are constructed of local travertine marble, and you can sit in cafes that haven't changed for a hundred years, built over the ruins of old Roman structures.

Old men sit out on their balconies smoking, drinking wine, and watching the passersby on the street below. Wouldn't you love to understand their bantering commentary? Street markets abound with fish, farm-fresh vegetables, and baked bread. Meals last forever, or seem to, with much laughter and conversation finished off with a shot of sambuca. It's very romantic, very peaceful. A sense of calm washes over you as you slow down to enjoy the moments of pleasure brought by a strong café and a small plate of tiny dolci (sweets).

Yet this rocky soil and mountainous region has also been an unforgiving landscape for past generations. Difficult to farm, with snow falling as late as June on occasion, this area my ancestors came from sent many of its inhabitants to America during the nineteenth century in hope of better opportunities, as did many countries.

It is interesting to reflect that the long, rocky road my ancestors traveled to find success in America was a loop I'd close with my own life's path, which has taken me from a fast-paced modern life back to my roots in Italy. I've come to embrace a lifestyle of slower, smaller pleasures: a glass of wine, a good cigar, a great cup of coffee. I'm enjoying every step along the way, including the opportunity to share this philosophy of life with you.

Writing this book has been one of my first four major life goals. The first goal was to get married and have kids because I love children and the joy of a full house.

The second goal was to get my MBA because I knew I wanted to be in business. I accomplished that just past my thirtieth birthday, right on target.

My third goal was to be my own boss and financially independent, owning a business that could produce income for me so that I could take time off without affecting operations. I wanted to achieve that by the time I was forty, and I thank God I did since it has allowed me immeasurable freedom to spend time with my family and my kids and to give them unforgettable experiences.

The last goal I set was to write my life story before I turned fifty. Though I have just reached the age of forty-three, I already have so much to write about that it's probably good I'm getting an early start.

My life story isn't just about me. It's about the people who have gone before me, whose examples inspired me to become an entrepreneur. It is about those who will follow, who I hope will be inspired to savor small privileges. It is about the mandolin moments in life that make fighting the wolves worth it.

During my career, I've served as the executive vice president for two nonprofit organizations. My father and I started a publishing venture that reprinted a historic treasure that has sold more than one hundred thousand copies in the past decade, and in 2007, I founded a media conglomerate that is now a five-year honoree on the *Inc.* 5000 List of America's Fastest-Growing Companies.

Along the way, I became more and more appreciative of life and the enjoyment of life's privileges. Inspired by mandolin echoes in the

Apennine foothills, I found my true calling in promoting a lifestyle that savors life's small moments: simple pleasures found in a good cup of coffee, a glass of great wine, the draw of a superb cigar. A new idea began to form in recent years: the Vallorani name as a brand. It makes perfect sense.

Companies work so hard to create marketing angles and stories around their brands. Yet here I am, with pages of stories to tell about my family heritage that tie back to our roots in Italy where the story of the wolves and the mandolin originated.

It is a privilege to be alive, to enjoy. Though life is full of wolves, it's up to us to find the music of the mandolin that calms them and keeps us sane. So now, I am building the brand, Vallorani Estates, to curate hand-selected, high-quality, boutique products that encourage the enjoyment of life's mandolin moments. My next life goal is to make Vallorani Estates a household name.

I came by my entrepreneurial drive naturally, as the stories I'm going to share with you will show. Everything I am I owe to those who went before, the courageous ones who faced hardships almost unimaginable to us today in order to come to America to make better lives for themselves and their families.

I find myself wanting to mirror Jack Welch's statement in *Straight from the Gut*: "Business is a lot like a world-class restaurant. When you peek behind the kitchen doors, the food never looks as good as when it comes to your table on fine china perfectly garnished. Business [and life] is messy and chaotic. In our kitchen, I hope you'll find something that might be helpful to you in reaching your own dreams."

When you look back in history and read these true stories that epitomize legend and lore, it is my hope you'll find how you too can keep the wolves at bay through the sweet strain of the mandolin. If they could do it, so can we!

What I Know to Be True

The world can be a cold, dark place full of hungry wolves biting at our ankles. Should we lock ourselves indoors and hide? No. We should pick up our mandolin and stride onward, bringing joy to our fellow travelers on this earth.

We must learn to find the moments in which we can enjoy life's privileges. It is up to us to take risks, reap the rewards, create beauty, and share the good we find with others.

CHAPTER ONE

"A PRETTY TOUGH GUY"

Behold, I send you out as sheep in the midst of wolves;
therefore be shrewd as serpents, and gentle as doves.

JESUS CHRIST

In his mellow old age, my late grandfather, Big D, enjoyed sipping a glass of wine and telling stories about his life and his father, Luigi. "Tell us about Luigi, Big D. Please tell us about Luigi," we'd beg him, like little kids, although by that time we were grown men.

He would pause, take a sip of wine, and look off into the distance, smiling at an old memory. A small appreciative laugh would follow. "He was a pretty tough guy, my dad," he'd say. "Luigi was pretty tough."

As you'll see from these stories handed down from my grandfather, Luigi was a pretty tough guy. His tender side came out when he was a much older man spending his days tending tomato plants. It is evidenced in his proud smile captured in a photo as he walked his two daughters down the aisle to get married on the same day.

But what my grandfather knew firsthand about his father concerned the *warrior* Luigi, the *immigrant* Luigi, and the *survivor* Luigi.

Originating in Italy, the name Luigi means "renowned fighter," a name my great-grandfather Luigi surely lived up to, though he was born Louis Vallorani. Traditional Italian naming practices would require that, as the second son, he be named for his maternal grandfather, who was still living. First sons were named for their paternal grandfather. It is quite common for nicknames to be used when so many of the same name live close together!

In those days very few had the means to own their own property and would, instead, tend the land of the wealthy for a share in the harvest. Though this feudal system began to disintegrate with the unification of Italy's provinces, just a generation before Luigi's birth, the majority of land was still owned by the wealthy and worked by those who were not wealthy.

Born to an impoverished farm family in the Marche Province, outside the small village of Offida, young Luigi vowed that he would not remain an uneducated poor farmer eking out a meager living among the rocky hills of his youth, struggling through life, always battling the wolves of hunger and low returns for his hard labor.

In 1911 the Ottoman Empire ruled great swaths of land in parts of Europe and North Africa. Boundary disputes and the ideological and religious differences of the Muslim Turks were considered great threats to the young Italian nation of Christians.

The Turks were proud of the inventive tortures they used on their helpless prisoners before "busting" them, one of the most barbaric and gruesome forms of execution, involving two swords cutting from shoulder to shoulder, beheading (or busting) the prisoner in the process.

As so many others of his generation had done, Luigi got his opportunity for adventure and heroism—and escape—when he was conscripted into military service to fight the Ottomans and their Muslim allies. After a brief military training, he found himself on a transport ship sailing to Libya where he would be a foot soldier in a hot, dusty invasion against Arab horsemen wielding swords.

At Benghazi and Sciara (Tripoli), bloody battles were fought. Thousands were lost. On one particular day, Luigi stood against charging horsemen and shot them one by one with his bolt-action rifle until he was trampled by the oncoming horses and rendered unconscious. When he came to, he found himself with a large group of other captured Italians, all of them bound and tied to boards as they waited to be sliced by Turkish swords.

Luigi watched grimly as the enemy gleefully and brutally killed the Italian survivors, one after another. Cursing and spitting at his captors, he prepared to die next. But just before the Turks could finish their bloodthirsty slaughter, an Italian counterattack halted the executions. Once freed, Luigi quickly recovered a weapon and charged back into the fray. I've always paused to consider how differently it could have gone. I wouldn't be here today if the timing had been just a little off!

Soon after, a peace treaty between the Ottoman Empire and Italy was established. The Ottoman troops agreed to remove themselves from Libya and allow Libya to remain under Italian oversight. It was a great victory for the Italians, who returned to Rome to march in a victory parade reminiscent of their ancient Roman forbearers.

The war over, Luigi set his sights on going where he believed the streets were paved with gold. He needed to find a way to sail for America. Like many young Italians of that day, Luigi thought of America as the Wild West—and he wasn't far from wrong.

In the early twentieth century, the Pittsburgh steel mills of western Pennsylvania had plenty of opportunities for newly arriving immigrants. Today, mere remnants of a bygone industry loom on the Monongahela riverside, but when Luigi arrived in McKeesport, Pennsylvania, it was the fastest-growing town in the country, with plenty of work in the steel mills for immigrants and ripe with possibilities for a young, entrepreneurially minded Italian. It was Luigi's goal from the beginning to work as a laborer only as long as it took to save enough money to start his own business.

He kept to himself, living in a boarding house and carrying with him his hard-earned money, at all times, to avoid having it stolen. One of the first purchases he made in America was a set of pearl-handled six-shooters, which he hid under his pillow in the room he shared with a roommate. What was his was his, and he intended to keep it that way.

He did not, at first, speak English very well but learned quickly and was soon able to distinguish English words well enough to understand conversations around him. It was because he was a sharp listener that he became aware of a plan his roommate was hatching with an accomplice to kill him and rob him of his hard-earned cash.

Thinking Luigi couldn't understand their English, the thieving, would-be killers made the mistake of talking about the plan in his presence. Luigi heard his roommate referring to the "dumb dago," and he began to eavesdrop on their plotting. His roommate planned to wait for him to fall asleep in their second-story room and then open a window to allow his accomplice to climb a ladder and enter the room. While the accomplice held Luigi down, the roommate would slit his throat and steal his stash of money. Both men would then flee out the window and down the ladder.

That night, Luigi feigned sleep with one of his loaded six-shooters clutched in his hand under the blanket. He listened intently as his roommate quietly opened the window to let in the accomplice climbing up the ladder. As soon as the climber's shoulders came through the open window, Luigi jumped up from his bed and shot the intruder point blank in the forehead, killing him instantly and sending his body and the ladder tumbling loudly to the ground below. Luigi then turned to his lunging roommate and pulled the trigger a second time, killing his would-be assassin. They had intended to show no mercy to Luigi, and Luigi showed none to either assailant. His descendants have owned one of the pearl-handled six-shooters to this day.

Even though he had killed in self-defense, Luigi knew he should slip away and go where people didn't know him. An old friend who had served with him in the war had also come to America and sought solace from his wartime memories by becoming a Catholic priest in a small Kentucky town. Luigi joined him there and quietly worked in a coal mine, saving every penny he could.

After a year, he felt it was safe to return to McKeesport. To serve the bustling Italian neighborhood there, he decided to open an Italian restaurant with the money he had been saving. One day, while he was strolling through the town, he heard a lovely girl named Maria DelMastro singing a beautiful song. Maria was a singer with a small band that performed in public parks where many immigrants and their families would gather to enjoy a pleasant Sunday afternoon. Luigi fell in love with Maria and, after obtaining permission from her father, married her.

Because Kentucky had less frigid winters than Pennsylvania and more opportunities to conduct business in less-crowded venues without as much competition, Luigi determined to sell his restaurant and return to Kentucky. One story has it that on the evening a prospective buyer came to investigate the restaurant, Luigi invited all of his friends to come in for a free meal. That night, the restaurant was crowded and bursting at the seams, so Luigi made the sale easily and headed for the hills with his wife and the two six-shooters to protect the cash he carried.

Once resettled in Kentucky, Luigi briefly went to work again as a coal miner in order to realize his latest dream of opening a grocery store. The hills surrounding the coal mines were notorious for murders and robberies in early twentieth-century Kentucky. Luigi, ever mindful of danger, carried his firearms strapped to his sides at all times. One morning, on his way to work in the predawn darkness, he encountered a would-be robber. Those pearl-handled pistols saved his life once again.

But fate dealt the young couple a tragic blow when their first child, only months old, took sick and died during a return visit to McKeesport in 1920. A second child born in Kentucky two years later died only eleven days after his birth. When Maria became pregnant a third time, she went back to McKeesport to stay with her family so she could have her mother and sister with her to help with the baby. Maria gave birth in July 1923 to Eugenio Vallorani, who survived to become my grandfather. Once again, a sobering thought of how precious life is: only one of three babies survived, and I would not be here today if he had not.

Luigi finally opened his grocery store. He had no pity for his competition. When the grocer across the road lowered prices to try and put Luigi out of business, Luigi sneaked across the street after dark and raised the prices back up on the chalkboard outside the man's store. Times were hard, and he had no qualms about doing whatever it took to keep his family fed and safe—to keep away the wolves baying at the door.

The wolves were never gone for long. Tragedy struck again when Maria died giving birth to a stillborn child in 1925. There seemed to be no peace in America, after all, and raising a child on his own was a daunting prospect. Tired of adventuring, and looking for a mother for his one surviving son, my grandfather, Luigi sold his store and took Eugenio back to McKeesport in the hope that Maria's family would care for him. Luigi had his heart set on returning to Italy. He wanted to marry an Italian woman, not an American woman, because he thought Italian women were less spoiled than American women.

When Maria's family couldn't agree to care for Eugenio for what would have been several years, likely because times were tough and he was so young and yet another mouth to feed, Luigi booked passage back to Italy for himself and his son.

Back in Italy, he settled in a farming community and used his American savings to buy farmland, vineyards, fruit orchards, and another grocery business. He found that Italian wife too. Agatha loved and cared for Eugenio, treating him as if he were her own son. And my grandfather loved his stepmother. Luigi and Agatha had three daughters—what a privilege it has been to meet two of them and their children and grandchildren. One of the daughters visited us in the USA in the 1980s, and another I met in Italy, twice, in 2011 and again in 2016.

Luigi never set foot in America again. We don't know why Luigi never came back to America. The year I was born, in 1973, he even applied for a US social security number from his home in Rimini, which suggests he meant to return, or at least to keep that possibility open. Whatever his reasons for choosing not to return, he certainly did not give up his entrepreneurial endeavors.

He achieved his goal of becoming a wealthy businessman and was greatly respected as the *padrone* of his village. He had true allegiance only to his family and those who depended on him. As he began to grow up and attend school, Luigi's young son was keenly aware of his father's status. Eugenio knew his father had big plans for him.

As Luigi's only son, Eugenio was also treated with respect in the village. When a fellow student bullied young Eugenio, Luigi went to the home of the bully's father and gave the father a choice: either the father would punish the bully, or Luigi would do it for him. The father punished his son right there in front of him rather than chance Luigi's temper.

On another occasion, during harvest season, young Eugenio was watching his father order one of the workers to stop his children from stealing fruit from the trees in his orchard. The worker made the mistake of picking up a clump of dirt and throwing it at Luigi in response. Luigi struck back by pummeling the recalcitrant worker. Then Luigi picked the man up, slung him over his shoulder, and carried him up a ladder with the apparent intention of throwing the disrespectful thief into the threshing machine. The other workers stopped Luigi before he did so, but the message was sent. Nobody stole his fruit after that.

Luigi disliked bullies, but during those days the biggest bullies of the twentieth century were rising in power: Adolph Hitler and Benito Mussolini. My grandfather was required to join a military youth group and was sent to march in a parade in support of Mussolini and Hitler. Luigi wanted no part of his son being pressed into the service of fascism. Having survived the horrors of his own wartime experience, Luigi was determined to keep Eugenio from the impending slaughter. He knew the only chance his son would have to avoid the political upheaval and ensuing bloody war was to be sent back to America to live.

The day of the big fascist parade in downtown Rome, Luigi watched reluctantly as young Eugenio marched. The boys extended their right arms straight out and saluted. It made Luigi disgusted to watch, so afterward, he proceeded directly to the US embassy and told the officials there how his boy had been born in Kentucky and was an American citizen, and he wanted to repatriate Eugenio in the US. He had Eugenio's birth certificate as proof and was able to get a US passport issued to him.

We still have that passport, and I have stood in front of that US Embassy in Rome. Seeing these places and knowing how important they were to my family's subsequent lives fills me with awe. How different history—my history—could have been had Luigi not been a "pretty tough guy."

Lighting one of his strong cigars, Luigi broke the news to his son that he was going to be sent to live with his mother's brothers in America. He was sitting by a fireplace and set his cigar on the mantle to stoke the fire. When he reached up to retrieve his cigar from the mantle, he accidentally picked up a scorpion lying there unnoticed beside his cigar.

Luigi immediately threw the venomous pest into the fire and realized he had been given the perfect example. He explained to his son why he was sending him back to America: As was the scorpion on the mantle, Mussolini and Hitler were both venomous men who would bring great harm. Until someone threw them into the fire, Luigi felt it best to protect his son by sending him back to Pennsylvania.

Fifteen-year-old Eugenio sailed to America on a ship called *The Rex*. There he became known as Eugene. It would be years before Eugene would get to see his father again. Because of the expense of the journey, they only saw each other twice again. In 1964 Eugene was able to return to Italy for one visit, and in 1972 he took his wife, my aunt, and my uncle and made another trip to Italy. Unfortunately, my father decided not to make the trip because he had just married my mother and felt the trip would be financially unwise. He has always regretted this decision.

Undefeated by thieves, killers, nations, and dictators, Luigi passed quietly in his sleep in Italy in February 1974, just a few months after my birth. While my father and I never got to meet Luigi in person, Luigi congratulated his son Eugene on the birth of a grandson (me). I cherish a letter he sent to my father prior to my birth, written in neat English.

In April 2016 I was able to visit Luigi's grave in Rimini, with his youngest daughter. At the age of eighty-three, Antonietta still tears up and lovingly whispers, "Papa Gi-Gi" as she crosses herself and touches her kissed fingers to a photo on his tomb.

His legacy lives on and inspires me to be a strong man, a sharp-thinking entrepreneur, and a protective father.

What I Know to Be True

Never give up. It took three tries for my great-grandfather to have a son who survived to carry on the Vallorani name. He never stopped trying to do more. While he did not settle in the United States to pursue the American dream for himself, he achieved it for his

family by planting the seeds of success. We reaped what Luigi sowed.

In business, you must be shrewd. In life, you should be prepared to defend yourself from all manner of wolves. Yet there is time to find moments of peaceful mandolin music in the enjoyment of a cigar or a glass of wine, and it is those moments that give us the stamina to continue the battle another day.

I subscribe to the Tarzan principle: Just keep swinging. The idea is to grab the next opportunity and keep swinging through the jungle. Following the example of my ancestors, I have used this principle many times in my life.

Despite the wolves in life—hardships, challenges, naysayers, even our own inner demons—we can enjoy the music of the mandolin, the good things in life. But nothing comes easy. We must have a vision, work hard, take risks, and make sacrifices. We don't talk about achieving it; we simply determine to achieve it. And we celebrate our victories with style.

That's where my brand comes into play: Vallorani Estates presents a lifestyle and curated products that are inspired by my family to bring melodious moments to your life to fight off life's wolves. Our philosophy is work hard, play hard. Be shrewd as a serpent, gentle as a dove, and survive as a sheep in the midst of wolves.

CHAPTER TWO

THE AMERICAN GENERATION

There are no constraints on the human mind, no walls around the human spirit, no barriers to our progress except those we ourselves erect.

RONALD REAGAN

My grandfather Eugene–Big D, as he was known to us growing up–returned to America at just fifteen years of age, having forgotten whatever English he'd known as a toddler, and was taken in by members of his mother's family. It was a lonely and difficult time for him. He was not guaranteed a warm and enthusiastic welcome. Times were tough, and another mouth to feed made things that much more difficult. Since he couldn't read or write English, he was remanded to the third grade.

Dominic DeDonato, my grandmother's brother, was his saving grace. I don't know how they met, but Uncle Dom took Eugene under his wing and would bring him home to eat with his family nearly every night of the week. Dom was a good-hearted, funny guy who was artistic and could draw very well. And he was smart. Dom eventually became a big boss at U.S. Steel in Philadelphia. In fact, my dad and my uncle Gene always referred to him as "Dom, the fox of industrial wizardry."

The DeDonatos had come to America at about the same time Eugene was going back to Italy as a boy and, as many had, Dom had found a home and work in western Pennsylvania steel country, eventually becoming a boss in the mills.

Eugene left his relatives' home as soon as he could, worked wherever he could, and at the age of nineteen, married Dom's sister Edith in the same church where Luigi had married Eugene's mother, Maria, years before.

My grandmother's given name was Italia, but Americans often mispronounced it as "EYE-talia," so one day in high school, she changed it to Edith after an American movie actress she admired, and she never looked back. She and my grandfather wanted to be Americans, 100 percent. She and Eugene had left the old country behind and wanted nothing more than to achieve the American dream. They weren't interested in being hyphenates.

During World War II, Eugene joined the US Army Air Corps and did his part for the war effort, and I find it ironic to think that he'd nearly been stuck on the other side of the conflict, back in Italy! Interestingly, in the lead-up to the war, he had been writing to his friends in Italy, not realizing that the US government was intercepting and reading his letters. There was nothing in them that suggested espionage or could have been considered a threat, just harmless stuff, just talking about his life in the United States.

Government agents approached him and asked, "Would you be willing to be a spy for the United States? We'll take you on a submarine off the coast of Italy, and you'll swim to shore. When you get to shore, your job is to just be an Italian. Sit in the bars, listen to the Germans and the Italians talking, and give us any information you can get back to us."

My grandfather said, "No, thank you. I don't want to die." As a uniformed US Army Air Corps man he was protected by the rules of war and would have been granted POW status if captured. As a spy, he could have faced summary execution with no trial beforehand, and possibly worse. He had a wife and a young son at this point and no desire to take such chances with their futures. Instead, he spent his war years in the South Pacific.

Eugene and Edith had three kids: my uncle Gene; my dad, Ray; and my aunt Linda. All three of the children became self-employed, successful entrepreneurs with close-knit families. I remember visiting my uncle Gene's house in Texas, as a teenager in 1992. He had a swimming pool and a smoker, and I watched him enjoy a cigar as he grilled a batch of steaks. Man, that was enjoying the good life! There are moments when you hear the sound of the mandolin and you never forget it. I knew at that moment this was the kind of life I wanted when I grew up.

My dad gave Eugene his lasting nickname, Big D, when he was a boy. Big D is short for Big Daddio. It fit him so well because not only was he a big strong guy but he also had a big strong personality and an even bigger heart.

There's one particular story about Big D I've always found inspiring. When the war was over, he returned home with his newfound engineering knowledge and went to work at a TV station in Pittsburgh. He was a technical engineer, making sure the radio station and TV station got on the air every morning. You had to have a first-class license with the FCC to do that job. But in 1955, this station was changing its systems, and everyone working for it was laid off.

All the men filed out and left, dejected, except Big D, who went back inside to say thank-you to the boss who had just laid him off for the opportunity to have worked there. Impressed by his gratitude, the boss gave Big D the name of a friend who worked at Westinghouse. Sometimes, there's a bump in the road, but if you do the right thing, it will iron itself out and you'll sail along again.

Eugene found himself employed at Westinghouse in 1955, with a large pay increase and a steady income that lasted until he retired. Suddenly, life wasn't quite as hard as it had been. The sweet melody of the mandolin was a little more frequent than the howling of the wolves at the door.

In 1979 Eugene was one of twenty-four who distinguished themselves apart from all others in the courageous defueling of the Three Mile Island nuclear-generating station in Dauphine County, Pennsylvania, where a partial nuclear meltdown had occurred. He was awarded a special commendation for preventing what could have turned into a disaster on the scale of Chernobyl. He mirrored his father, Luigi, in demonstrating bravery and courage in the face of adversity.

During my adult years, I became closer to Big D every year, partly because I was getting older too and recognizing the inevitability of my own mortality. In 2011 my grandmother Edith passed at the age of eighty-eight. She was such a spry, sharp, strong woman that when she died I was completely taken off guard. I hadn't seen it coming.

My grandfather loved her so much. When I saw him at the funeral, kissing her picture and tearing up, I wanted to bring him some joy, to give him something to look forward to, and I thought, *We're going to Italy.* I was watching the end of an era, and I knew that my grandfather wouldn't live forever.

That September, my dad, my brother, my grandfather, and I visited Italy. My father, brother, and I got to meet Luigi's family for the first time. Big D translated, and some of my cousins worked on their English skills with us. It was an amazing trip, and it was in Italy in 2011 that I began to realize one of my missions in life would be to make the Vallorani name a legacy.

Between 2011 and 2016, when Big D passed away, I asked him as many questions as I could, often filming our chats for posterity. I frequently asked his advice on life, and his perspective was always interesting to me. He would often sing a little Italian tune, with a bit of coaxing, and he loved to talk.

He had the most beautiful handwriting I've ever seen, and he used to draft electrical plans that were very impressive to me, as a kid. He was very adept with computers. He worked in DOS and Windows. Then he really wanted an iPad. He couldn't understand how the touch screen would work for him, but he knew he wanted one because it was the newest thing.

Big D was a fastidious guy. He didn't drink water, even with his pills. "Just coffee and wine," he'd say jovially, and those beverages were all he would accept. He'd drink cups of strong black coffee until noon, when he'd switch to red wine.

For his ninetieth birthday in 2013, we threw a massive party at my home outside Atlanta. We flew him in from Pittsburgh, and most of the family was able to come together from across the country to celebrate. I drank vodka because it has lower calories, and I thought it was healthier than wine. My grandfather just shook his head. "You should be drinking wine. You're putting nails in your coffin." But later on, when he saw me drinking a vodka martini, he was okay with that. Somehow, calling it a martini made it acceptable. Following his advice, I have gone back to preferring Italian wine.

I got my passion for family history from Big D. He preserved all the eight-millimeter home movies and showed us old family films going way back. Every Christmas time, we'd watch them. He documented a lot of family history, including his visits back to Italy to see Luigi. To this day, I cannot hold back tears as I watch the film of my grandfather Eugene hugging his father, Luigi, in 1972. He didn't know it would be the last time.

One last story: In the 1960s my grandfather wanted to find the grave of his mother, Maria, in Kentucky. He took my dad and my aunt Linda, both young children at the time. They searched and asked the caretaker of the cemetery, but nobody could help them to find Maria's grave. I don't know if you've ever tried to find the grave of an ancestor. You walk and you walk, checking headstone after headstone, many so worn with age they are nearly impossible to read. It's very frustrating.

After fruitless hours of walking around, trying to locate the grave, they got back in the car, defeated, and started to drive back home. As they were driving through the cemetery to the exit, the car stalled. They got out to see what the problem was, and just beside them was my grandmother's grave. I know this sounds incredible, but my dad tells me to this day he remembers it clearly.

They paid their respects and said their prayers and got back in the car, and—wouldn't you know—the car started up fine, and they drove away with no problem. They had the car checked out by a mechanic, who found not a thing wrong with it.

One of Big D's last sentiments as he neared the day of his passing was that he would soon get to see his father, Luigi, and his wife, Edith, again, and that he would get to meet his mother, Maria.

Big D had a quality that's pretty rare today in that he was truly content with life. With him, everything was always "pretty good" or "not too bad." During his last week of life, when he was in the hospital, he'd call me and tell me about all the nice things they had for him there. "I got a TV and a couch to sit on. It's pretty good."

He never saw the wolves as subjects to focus on and would choose, instead, to enjoy the small moments that make life beautiful. He'd share stories with me about his dad, Luigi, how they'd make wine together, and how much Luigi enjoyed smoking a leisurely cigar. Big D would sing a simple tune in Italian, and I could almost see his smile over the phone.

My grandfather's pleasure in the simple things in life—a good cup of coffee, a good glass of wine—has inspired me to make an effort to enjoy and share the simple things with others. One person I particularly enjoy spending time with is my own dad. I am very grateful to have a great relationship with both my parents.

My dad was born in 1949, a typical, all-American, baby-boomer boy. He played baseball, followed the Pittsburgh Pirates, and spoke only English. Though he heard his relatives speak Italian occasionally, Dad never was taught to speak it. He grew up with Jewish boys and Irish boys. He attended an Irish Catholic Church. The idea of identity politics didn't exist then as it does today, and kids from all backgrounds enjoyed playing together.

All of my relatives on both sides of my family had a strong religious faith. I believe that God has blessed our family because of this faith. If I were ever to walk away from the Church, which would be unthinkable, I would be letting down generations of devout people who went before me. My dad was an altar boy and went to mass every Sunday with his family. It was a big deal.

Even though her ancestors were Lutheran, my mother never missed a Sunday service at the local Baptist church. Her father had taught her that you should support your community church, regardless of the denomination. That open-minded view made a huge impression on me and taught me tolerance. All the way down, on both sides, it was expected that the family would worship together in church every Sunday.

My mother emphasized morality, but we were far from perfect. That's why we had faith in the one who was perfect on our behalf. Faith is a big part of who I am and what I want to pass on to my kids. It could all stop with me, as it has with a lot of people in my generation, but if I didn't make faith an important part of my kids' lives, then I'd have failed to pass on important values.

I remember learning that my first best friend was an atheist and being completely caught off guard by that: "What? You're an atheist? What is that?" It was a foreign concept to me because I'd been around religion my whole life. It was just a part of who we were, in a quiet, all-encompassing way.

All of our family has been private about our faith. We were never ones to take to the streets to preach at people. I don't go around beating people over the head with my particular political or religious views. If somebody is interested and we want to talk about it, we can. It's never "Let me tell you what I think, why you're wrong and I'm right." Nobody in our family ever did that. It would have been considered rude. If people were drawn into our way of life, it was more because of what they saw than what we said.

In fact, that atheist friend of mine ended up converting to Christianity and even worked for my business for several years. I think that's the way our family would have liked it—that people just saw what we had and wanted to share in it too.

My dad was a go-getter with a gift for words. As a teenager, he started a radio station in his dad's garage, no doubt in violation of

FCC rules, but that's how it goes when your dad's an engineer. That was the beginning of his love for working in media.

My dad lived in Liberty Borough, which was a community of McKeesport. When he went to college in the city of Pittsburgh, even though they worked at bigger broadcast stations in Pittsburgh, guys would come over to his garage to do broadcasts because they were his friends. They'd play top-forty hits, just as they did at the stations where they worked. At that same time, my dad read the news for a college station in Pittsburgh. That college campus station, WPPJ, is still active in downtown Pittsburgh.

A friend of my dad's, who had press passes because he worked for a TV station in Salisbury, Maryland, came back to Pittsburgh for the weekend. "I've got press passes for the Pirates baseball game," he said and invited my dad to go with him. Dad was thrilled because he got to walk around on the field and interview players and go up into the press box. It's what he'd always wanted to do, and he didn't waste his time when he got there.

When he got up into that press box, he asked the reporters there if they knew of anyone who was quitting a newspaper job. One guy said, "Yeah, I know a guy that's quitting. Here's my boss's name. Call him up."

When Dad got home, he immediately called the man's boss and was invited to "come up for an interview." That got Dad his first real newspapering job at one of the oldest papers in Pennsylvania, *The Bedford Gazette*. He went on to work for the NBC affiliate television station where he wrote stories and was an announcer for weather, news, and sports.

His brother, Gene, lured him out of the TV business and back into the newspaper industry. Gene wanted my dad to help out with photography, sports, and news for his paper, *The Central West Virginia*

Guardian. After a few years, Dad decided to start a business of his own. He and a business partner started a weekly classifieds publication that he owns and operates to this day.

For whatever reason, it was very common for Pittsburgh men to marry West Virginia women. They would go across the Mason-Dixon line and find themselves a southern girl. My uncle Gene was the first to do this in our family, moving to West Virginia where he met and married my aunt Trina.

Trina and my mom grew up next door to each other. It was my Aunt Trina's idea to try to fix up my mom, Linda Burgreen, with her husband's little brother, Ray, who was living with them for the summer. While they were spending a leisurely evening at home, my mom would "pop in randomly" to visit Trina. When she arrived, Trina would "casually" introduce Ray and Linda to each other.

I heard that seconds after my parents met in this manner, Linda and Trina had to rush off, giggling, into one of the other rooms as they could hardly contain themselves long enough to get the "accidental meeting" pulled off.

It wasn't love at first sight, my mom told me, but they liked each other enough to start dating and would go out to the movies or to Dairy Queen. My dad was a nice-looking and sincerely nice guy—and still is! Over time, Mom fell in love with him, and they got married. My parents have had a strong marriage.

Once married, they moved to Clarksburg, West Virginia, where I was born in 1973. Now, an interesting thing about Clarksburg is that it has a massive Italian American population. While a lot of the Italian immigrants went to work in the steel mills of Pittsburgh, two hours south, in Clarksburg, many found work in the coal mines.

Clarksburg still has some of the best Italian restaurants you'll ever find. As an Italian from Pittsburgh, my dad fit in really well.

The thing I love about Clarksburg is they have a big Italian heritage festival every year. They even crown one of the little girls *Regina [Queen] Bellissimo [Beautiful]!*

Clarksburg is also known as the birthplace of General Stonewall Jackson. I have a lot of respect for Stonewall and even named one of my sons, Levi Jackson, after him. Though a staunch Confederate, he was not a slave owner, nor did he believe in slavery. In fact, he opened schools for African Americans and taught them to read outside the laws of the day.

This particular story about Jackson inspires me. It's one I've heard and read many times:

> During the heat of the battle (1st Manassas) a messenger came and handed Jackson a letter to sign. He dismounted just as a canon ball blew up a tree nearby. Wood chips rained down on Jackson but, without missing a beat, he calmly brushed the wood chips from the paper and continued reading. He then got back on his horse as though nothing unusual had happened. Those around him were astonished at his composure. Someone spoke up and asked him how he could be so cool.
>
> Jackson replied, "My religious belief teaches me to feel as safe in battle as in bed. God has fixed the time for my death. I do not concern myself about that, but to be always ready, no matter when it may overtake me . . . That is the way all men should live, and then all would be equally brave." His cool fearlessness in the heat of battle earned him his nickname. It was, reportedly, General Bee, who during a charge at first battle of Manassas, cried to his frightened

men, "Look, there stands Jackson like a stone wall." And the battle was won.[1]

To this day, in the town of Clarksburg, there's a giant monument to Stonewall Jackson and a state park called Jackson's Mill. His life was an example of morality and bravery that no matter where you stand politically or historically, you have to admire him for the man he was. When Stonewall Jackson faced the wolves, he chose the peace of God over fear.

Even though our first family home was a single-wide trailer, there was no way someone as smart and industrious as my dad would let us linger there for long. He juggled multiple jobs, always trying to get ahead. At various times, he was a sports writer for a newspaper, a TV weatherman at WBOY in Clarksburg, and a guard at a reform school.

My father's big success came from starting the business he still owns today, Photo Craft Corporation. Photo Craft publishes a buy/sell/trade publication that is just a little bit younger than I am. This newspaper is what, basically, funded our family through my childhood, though in the early days my dad moonlighted as a wedding photographer to keep us afloat.

He still made time to be with Mom and us kids, though, even swapping ad space for motel rooms so we could go on vacations together. My dad read us a Bible story every night, and he was very involved in our lives. He taught me how to chop firewood and how to grow vegetables in our family's garden. He always had time to throw a baseball with me.

1 "Stonewall Jackson," Wikipedia, https://en.wikipedia.org/wiki/Stonewall_Jackson.

Family has always been a priority for my dad, just as it has been for me. My dad is even more of a mentor to me now than he was when I was younger.

He and my mother were determined their children would have the best of everything. My mother, in particular, wanted us to be well dressed and confident in our appearances. Both of my parents did everything they could to give us the best childhood possible and to instill in us the values they had learned from their hard-working families.

My mom hated any kind of conflict in the house. She had very high standards for herself and for us kids and taught us to bring our best efforts to everything we did. She had been the very first college graduate in her own family and carefully monitored all of our homework, handing it back to us for revisions if it wasn't up to snuff.

"Good enough" wasn't good enough. You had to do your best, every time. No surprise that my siblings and I were all honor students. The collection of trophies for my wins at spelling-bee championships was impressive, and I was a straight-A student all through high school, slated for salutatorian of our class. When we merged with another school in my senior year, a girl from the other school was valedictorian, so I was bumped to third in my class. She had survived a recent car accident involving a drunk driver, and her speech at graduation made a profound impact on our entire school.

I attribute much of my success in life, now, to my mom's driving me through my childhood. She believed in us with all her heart and instilled her own can-do confidence in us. In everything I attempted and every challenge I took up, she was my tireless cheerleader. She thought of me as her golden boy and poured a tremendous amount of love, energy, and enthusiasm into everything I did. My mom wasn't just tough but also very sensitive, and she would talk me through problems, guiding me through adolescence. I don't think I ever came home from a date or an activity without talking it all out with her. Having that open communication with my parents was something I really appreciated. It hasn't changed though I'm in my forties. I still call home to hear their opinions and garner advice.

Her family was entrepreneurial too, hard-working immigrant stock from the Scandinavian region. On my mom's side, my great-great-grandfather was a farmer, but unlike other farmers, he sold directly to the consumer when all the farmers around him were selling wholesale. He grew vegetables, raised chickens for eggs, kept cows, and took all that he produced to the city himself to sell at higher retail prices. He also delivered fresh milk from his dairy to people's houses. My grandfather says they always had good food to eat.

One thing that impressed me from stories passed down was that if they had a bad crop year, he always had saved enough so that they could get through the tough time. As my grandfather Hartley put it, they not only anticipated bad years but survived bad years well. He told me, "I don't know any businessman that hasn't had a bad time or a lean year. It hits us all."

Rather than going into the farming business, my grandfather Hartley—Pap—owned and operated his own tractor-trailer. My Pap has a sense of humor that rivals few, and he's always ready to share a story everyone will laugh over. We go so quickly through life, nowadays, and often feel the pressure of the wolves dogging our heels. Humor, storytelling, and passing down family legends are important ways to slow down so we can savor the haunting melody of the mandolin.

America is a diverse country built by immigrants. In Luigi's era, you sailed over, were processed quickly upon arrival, and were immediately considered an American. You would learn as you went forward. Somehow, we've lost that simplicity. I don't think many political groups have properly articulated a good plan for immigration. We need to make it easier for people to make a life here.

Neither Republicans nor Democrats seem to deliver a balanced perspective on immigration.

To elaborate: My perception is that the Democratic Party essentially says, "Open up the floodgates. We'll give amnesty to everybody. Pour in because we want your vote. Latch on to the entitlement society that we have. We'll take care of you." Immigrants are offered an easy street by the Democrat platform, which is a major disservice to them. As the old saying goes, "Give a man a fish, and he'll eat for a day. Teach a man to fish, and he'll eat for a lifetime."

The Republican Party perspective can be almost xenophobic: "Stop. We don't want your language here. I don't want to press one for English. Stay away, or only come in after you fill out this paperwork—and wait three years."

I've known people from all parts of the world—not just Latin America but also Ireland, Australia, and Canada—who simply cannot start a new life in this country despite the value they could bring. It's virtually a miracle to immigrate legally. The rules are very different from what they were in Luigi's time. Many don't have the luxury of waiting for mounds of paperwork and red tape to be processed. They may be struggling to survive.

Today, two different attitudes are exhibited. There are many working hard to make a good life here. They brought with them solid family values and a strong work ethic. They have hopes of achieving the American dream for themselves and their children. Then there are some who sadly see the American dream as merely a place where everything should be free and handed to them by the government.

None of my ancestors would have taken a dollar from the government or charity. It would have been against their principles. Their attitude was, "No thanks. We earn our own, and we take care of our own. If we face wolves, we'll figure out how to play the mandolin anyway."

I think we've lost a lot of that sense of self-reliance, particularly among the younger generation. There's a pervasive sense of entitlement that I find very distressing.

People can achieve anything they put their mind and effort toward. I would welcome people to this country, legally, with simple requirements: they must understand our form of government, commit to learning English, and integrate into our society.

Our country is as strong as it is today because people like my immigrant ancestors risked everything to come here and were more than willing to work hard to make their dreams come true. I believe this attitude is what makes—and keeps—our country great.

What I Know to Be True

I owe so much of who I am to my parents and to the values they instilled in me, both through what they said and, more importantly, what they did.

My mom made me believe I could accomplish anything. She expected me to do my best, and I was eager to live up to her expectations because there was so much love implicit in them. My dad's example as a small-business owner inspired me as well.

Both of them are devout Christians—my dad was raised as a Roman Catholic and my mother as a Protestant—so I was raised in a very moral home with a strong work ethic.

Without those tools—love, faith, and willingness to take on a tough job—I'd not have enjoyed the successes I have. I'd rather leave my kids a legacy of solid values than of merely money.

CHAPTER THREE

———————◆———————

THE EDUCATION OF AN ENTREPRENEUR

A man who doesn't spend time with his
family can never be a real man.

MARIO PUZO, *THE GODFATHER*

My parents recognized my artistic talent at a very early
age and paid for me to take private art lessons for years.
I learned oil painting, charcoal sketching, pen-and-ink
drawing, and so forth. All of my friends called me "the artist" and
expected that was what I would be when I grew up. But as much as
I loved it, I knew I didn't want to be a starving artist. So my dad had
me watch training videos on graphic design by Jan V. White. Those
videos had a real impact on me.

At fifteen years of age I went to work for my dad's business after
school, full-time, through the summers and in between my classes at
West Virginia University (WVU), post high school.

Working for my dad in his entrepreneurial endeavors was great.
At first, I just did whatever odd jobs needed to be done. Sometimes,
he would hand me the car keys and I would wash and detail all the
company cars for the sales department. Other times, I was planting

THE WOLVES & THE MANDOLIN

and maintaining the landscaping around the office, keeping the office looking good. These kinds of chores were my work for the first couple of years.

However, Dad always knew I could do much bigger things. Soon I was promoted to ad design and page layout. At that time, layout was a much more hands-on affair than it is today, when everything is done on a computer. It was a blend of computer layout and the old-fashioned, paste-up method of putting a newspaper together. We literally pasted blocks of text, articles, and advertisements on a piece of grid paper. The newspaper was between 88 and 112 pages, so it was fairly labor intensive. Also during this period I learned the basic principles of effective marketing.

One of the best things about working with my father was that he'd take me to business meetings, even when I was a kid. I'd suit up in my tie and jacket, and I learned how to behave in a business setting with other adults. I've always felt that gave me a real advantage when I entered the business world. A lot of my friends were baggers at the grocery store at that age, whereas I was out there in the corporate world, observing successful businessmen, sitting at the table with them, and hearing them and my dad talk real business.

In these settings, without even trying, I absorbed a lot about business, especially about running one. It wasn't as though my dad said, "Okay, son, here's a lesson for you." I just saw it play out in front of me and took it all in. I learned a lot about image, leadership, management, hierarchy, employees, and money. I remember thinking how distinguished all of these businesspeople looked, and I wanted to be like them. I wanted to be a businessman someday and own my own business. They all inspired me. It was a tremendous education.

As common as blue-collar work was in West Virginia, I never saw myself as a blue-collar guy. As much as I looked up to my maternal grandfather, I couldn't see myself driving a truck. Being very patriotic, I even considered joining the military. However, I felt my real calling was going to be found in the corporate world, where marketing, idea development, and creating something new could provide an ample living.

I learned so much from my father, not the least of which was how to be a good boss. My dad never raised his voice at an employee. He led (and still does to this day) by inspiration and kindness. People want to please my dad. They don't fear him; they love him. He's achieved that balance everywhere he's ever been. Even when he was a guard at the boys' reform school, the boys there loved him. I do not think my dad has a single enemy in the world. At least, I have yet to find one.

Something else that I learned from my father was to never owe my boss. As an employee, I have always had the attitude that I wanted my boss to owe me, not the other way around. I always worked more hours than I was paid for and made an effort to be available at all times. It was important to me that I went the extra mile so my boss felt he had to take care of me and give me a raise and some time off. Because of this extra-mile attitude, I found myself being rewarded throughout my career.

Likewise, as a boss, I am dedicated to being generous to my employees. I'm proud that they often go the extra mile for me. I have always had several who stay late to work on a project or work an extra day because they desire to please me and get the results I've requested. When employers are indebted to their employees, they get the pleasure of rewarding those employees for their attitude.

When I have to lay off employees, I always give a generous severance payment, which is not something my ancestors would have understood. Unfortunately, many employees in today's world believe

41

they are owed the severance pay. They're not. They already got paid for the services they provided. Severance means employees are paid for services they didn't get to provide. I try to go above and beyond by giving them a chance to get up and running somewhere else.

If, rather than exhibiting a sense of entitlement, employees were to express gratitude for the employment opportunity, as my grandfather did when he was let go, many could find themselves swinging to a new and better opportunity.

Big D didn't ask for a dollar more, and he didn't get severance pay. But his attitude did win him the admiration of his ex-boss and the help he needed to get his next job at Westinghouse. What do you think was worth more in the long term? He made his boss feel indebted—to a degree.

That's what I would recommend to people who work for someone else. Go over and above what you're called to do. Don't always be looking for quid pro quo. Don't say, "It's not my job," or "It's not my problem." As expressed by the adage that "the cream rises to the top," those who are willing to work hard and go the extra mile are usually more successful in life and business.

Employees should also seek to be not only indispensible but also introspective. They should ask themselves what their skills and weaknesses are, and they should be honest with themselves and seek improvement in areas that need it. Most people who are fired don't seem to understand why they were fired, although everyone around them may have complained for months about their behavior or about their attitude.

My COO, Liz, is an example of someone who gives everything she has to her job and more. She started off in customer service before becoming my executive assistant. I needed her to handle the bookkeeping in one of my divisions, so she did it. Then I asked her to be our director of human resources. Now she's my COO, helping me run the entire Vallorani Estates brand and making a nice salary. She's just pushed and pushed and pushed.

My CFO, Tracey, often works long into the night and on weekends to ensure my companies are on track financially, and to deliver necessary reporting to our clients. Jared, my CEO, is available 24-7 to solve problems, manage multiple projects, and streamline operations.

Many people will never climb their organization's ladder, because they won't invest enough of their time and make an effort to stand out from the pack. They're clock-punchers, in at 9:00 a.m., out at 5:00 p.m. "Oh, you need me to do something extra? I want overtime," they may say, or "I want a day off." They'll even say, "That's not in my job description."

In my company, people with that attitude never go very far. They either keep the job they're in for years, or they move elsewhere. But for people who put in the effort, there's no ceiling. Eventually, Liz, Tracey, and Jared became business partners in my various endeavors because their attitude matched their ambition. That's how my grandfather prospered too.

I was raised in a very moral home with a strong work ethic. If I learned anything from my family's example and the examples of those who'd gone before, it is that it's a privilege to be alive and to be able to work hard to make a good life. Despite the wolves in life, hardships, challenges, naysayers, and even our own inner demons, we can enjoy the music of the mandolin. It's a privilege just to get up in the morning and take a breath, to enjoy life, to sip a cup of great coffee, or to toast with a divine wine over a long dinner with friends.

These simple yet profound pleasures are privileges, not rights. We are not entitled to anything. We work hard to earn such pleasures, and we should learn to appreciate them and enjoy sharing them with others around us.

Nothing worth having comes easily. Nobody hands anything to us. We have to have a vision to accomplish our aims. We have to work hard. We have to take risks. We have to make sacrifices. We can't just talk about achieving. Marcus Aurelius said, "Don't talk about what being a good man is. Be one." Don't talk about what you're going to do. Do it. Just start. It's never too early, and it's never too late.

Another thing I learned from my family is to celebrate every victory with style, and that's one thing I've tried to carry forward in my business and in my family. I remember when we paid off our house mortgage, I brought my kids together, cracked open a bottle of prosecco, and said, "Okay guys, I want to let everybody know that we just paid off the house!" It was a special moment.

If you don't take time out to celebrate those special little moments, even if it's just surviving an especially challenging day of work, you're cheating yourself of that victory. Seek to always find a victory to celebrate: "I accomplished five important things in my work or home life today. Now I'm going to pour myself a glass of wine and admire the sunset."

Some people are workaholics and proud of it. I work extremely hard, but I believe in playing hard too. It takes effort to pause, smell the roses, play ball with my boys in the backyard, read to my youngest kids, tuck them in at night, and enjoy a good movie with the family. And it's the best effort I am privileged to give.

There's nothing better than sitting down to a freshly grilled steak on the patio and lighting up a great cigar as the moon rises over the tree line. Listening to some good tunes while I sip a glass of wine with my family reminds me of why I work hard. These are the privileges of life, these small moments.

If you find you are not taking the time to experience these moments in your life, what can you do to change? What is the point of all this hard work to keep the wolves at bay if you're not enjoying the music of the mandolin?

Vallorani Estates promotes hard work but also encourages people to achieve enjoyment in life. Take the time to slow down and enjoy life's privileges. Don't let the wolves overtake you. And don't die with nothing more than a big fat bank account. What good does that do?

If I die with a massive bank account, I've never enjoyed that money. If I didn't spend it on my kids and take hunting trips with them, for instance, what am I going to leave them? Just a big pile of money they're likely to perpetuate? They're not going to spend it on making memories with their kids, either. Two or three generations later, we'll get a kid who blows through it all. That's not what taming life's wolves should mean.

I love taking my kids on hunting trips. It takes several thousand dollars to make these trips, between airfare, lodging, guides, and the taxidermy afterward. People tell me I could have invested that money elsewhere. I could have bought this or that stock or put the money into my retirement account.

But for me, there's no better way to spend my money than to create memories with my kids and spend time with them. I teach them how to be patient and wait for the right shot and to feed hungry children with the meat we donate from the hunt. We spend solid hours together and display the trophies in our home, a constant reminder of the skills we achieved through that trip. Those are some of our best memories. How can you put a price on that?

At WVU, I picked graphic design for my major because I felt it was a way to apply my artistic skills and talents to making a living. I also liked the fact that it had a business side to it. As a graphic designer, I put together advertisements, book covers, and posters. And graphic design utilized computers, another plus for me. The fine arts are the old-fashioned media, whereas graphic design harnesses the same creativity with a modern tool. However, I look forward to picking up a paintbrush again some day.

Our graphic-design professor put our work up on the wall from the first class, and mine came in dead last. I thought it was because my last name is Vallorani and she'd alphabetized. But no. She had put up our work in the order of best to worst. Mind you, this wasn't my first experience with design. I had been a student of art for years and had already started creating display advertising, professionally, in my dad's business.

This kind of thing could be discouraging to a lot of students, but to me, it was motivating. When I came in last, I told myself I'd never be last again. Consistently, after that first time, my assignment projects placed first, or were among the five best, and I was soon at the top of my class.

Unlike much of fine art, graphic design isn't subjective. There are rules. Typography, lines, texture, white space—all of it matters. My professors gave us very specific assignments, such as how to draw perfect curves by hand. If we didn't follow the instructions exactly, we were graded down. It was a real critique. We had to adhere to the elements of graphic design and create according to the rules. That was valuable education I've used through most of my business life.

I will also never forget my photography professor. He gave us an assignment to go out and take pictures at random for an entire day. I'm a very efficient person, so I took that assignment, thinking I'd take twenty-four pictures—one roll of film—and I'd be done quickly. The next day I turned in my twenty-four photos.

My professor just stared at me. "That's it? Those are all the pictures you took?" His look said it more clearly than words could have. He was implying that the height of arrogance is to think of getting the perfect shot with only one roll of film. He expected us all to come in with rolls and rolls of printed shots. But I had a job, and I had all these classes—and the pictures I had taken were actually pretty good.

That wasn't the point, of course, and I learned a big lesson in humility that day. Getting the perfect composition required effort, time, and attention to detail. It required pushing harder than I thought I could push. I gained a better understanding of what it was to look at everything in life through a new pair of eyes and to search to find the best artistic portrayal.

One piece of advice I received in that program has always stayed with me: my teachers told me to never apologize for my artwork. A local bank had our class design its new logo, and out of the entire class, my design was chosen. As part of the competition, I had to do a presentation in front of a group of bankers and businesspeople.

I remember my teacher telling me during the process, "Don't get up there for your presentation and say, 'I was up late last night. I've been really busy. I'm not sure I did this how you wanted. This is not my best work.' Don't make excuses. Just deliver it."

It was great advice. If you say something negative, you encourage agreement. If you put yourself down, people might believe you! Why not simply stand up and say, "Here is my music." Period. Don't apologize or make excuses.

During my sophomore year, I met my future wife, Jan, through a campus Christian group. Her older sister was also a member of the group, and on Valentine's Day, we played a dating game. Jan's older sister somehow rigged it to make me the bachelor who won so Jan and I could go on a date. We got married while we were still in college, the summer before our senior year.

One important thing Jan and I had in common is that we both wanted children. She would have been content with three, but we ended up having seven: three girls and four boys. That's because I think big and I wanted to extend the Vallorani name in a big way, and I love the joy of a full house.

Before we were married, we planned to homeschool our children. Having the flexibility that homeschooling gives allows us to take the kids on life experiences that are extended field trips: traveling the US and abroad, hunting, fishing, camping, visiting historic sites, museums—these kinds of things. Jan had gained valuable experience in teaching while she was earning her degree in elementary education. We're currently part of a hybrid system in which our children are partly homeschooled and partly educated in a co-op. Classical Conversations gives kids a classical education while they are exposed to tutors and teachers other than their mother. Jan teaches one of these classes.

We were able to take our two oldest on a Mediterranean cruise to Italy, Spain, and France a couple of years ago. My daughter and I have hunted boar together, and my sons and I have had several hunting trips over the years. With trips to Plymouth Rock and

Caribbean plantations and beach trips with the extended family, our life has been rich with happy moments because of the freedom homeschooling provides.

Why We Homeschool

Homeschooling was always our first choice, and it's come a long way since it was first legalized. While there are some great teachers in the public schools, I do not always agree with the curriculum that is being taught today. First of all, much of the curriculum is built on atheistic philosophy and teaches that the state is the solution to society's problems. Second, the promotion of socialism over capitalist ideology is alarming. Third, America's great history and foundational principles have been largely ignored or totally rewritten.

My kids are fortunate their mom is their teacher, but they are not limited to just one person. Our kids are exposed to other adults as authority figures because they have always been involved in my business. They sit and listen when I have business guests join us for dinner and cigars. My older kids have traveled with me on business trips. They never developed the "youth-supremacy" mind-set that so many kids have today, in which authority is incessantly questioned. Interaction with other adults is a part of their everyday life, and they learned to converse with adults at an early age.

Unlike some homeschooling families, however, we are a family that watches films and listens to all types of music together. I want to expose them to other worldviews and help them understand why we believe what we do. They get a plethora of outside lessons too: sports, dance, music, art, martial arts, and so forth. I think we have been able to bring the best of both worlds together. It fits our lifestyle beautifully. We can just pick up and drive off in the RV and still homeschool according to our family values. They get experiences that few kids have the opportunity to enjoy.

During my final year at WVU, I interned in the printing and communications division, so I got to work in all aspects of the printing press—prepress, photolithography, press, and bindery, something I really enjoyed. A couple of months after I graduated and finished my internship, I went back to work at my dad's company. Then my former boss called me from the school printing shop. The head of the department had gotten ill and I was told they really needed me back.

True to my nature, I was overly optimistic about my pay from my dad. I thought my dad was paying me $10 an hour. When the school officials offered me $10.25 an hour, I went to my dad for advice. "Hey, Dad, the university called me back and they're going to pay me 25 cents more an hour than you're paying me." He said, "$8.75?" I said, "No, $10.25 an hour." He said, "No, Son, that's a couple more dollars an hour than what I'm paying you!" He urged me to take the opportunity.

My first job outside the family business was paid at that rate: a good bit of money in those days! It was great. We had a classified column for university jobs that I got first crack at since I was publishing it. I was always scanning for graphic design jobs, especially for ones that might promise even better opportunities.

One day, the opportunity came. It was a position with a higher rate of pay, as a salary with benefits, which was a big step up for me from an hourly rate. So I transferred to the extension service, a state-run entity within the university that sent experts into the field to work with farmers, breeders, and others in agriculture.

For two years, I worked there as a graphic designer and did web work too. That's really where I first got experience with the Internet. We had to have a website, so I learned how to make GIFs and JPEGs and write HTML. I think we even did e-mail blasts, or at least an early version of them.

After about two years, I felt I'd done all I could in my job at the university. It is a state-run institution, which means budget limitations. A lot of the publications were in black and white. The paper selection was lean. Other than the web work, I found myself, in my second year, producing somewhat dull government pamphlets. I wanted to get into the private sector, make more of myself, and do more with my skills.

People around me were making more money, which motivated me. My sister-in-law was working in IT at a law firm. She would tell us she just got a $5,000 bonus. What? That was one-fifth of my annual salary! I had many great ideas about what I could do with $5,000. My brother-in-law had a music degree and was working at a tech company that provided cybersecurity. I didn't really know what he did, but I knew he was making good money. That is when I started feeling the itch to move on and realize my potential in a new career path.

What I Know to Be True

My art professor's advice to me has continued to help me throughout my life: never begin by apologizing for your work. If you're going to give a speech or a presentation or hand someone a resume—whatever it is—face your clients or your employer or potential employer and let them know, "You're getting my absolute best. This is my top work." People will believe you. If you start apologizing and make excuses, you're setting them up to see a weakness or a failure.

There is, obviously, a time when you need to be honest or humble, but that's not what I'm talking about here. When you're self-deprecating while trying to sell something or close a deal or while giving a speech or presentation, it's a turn-off. People will see flaws after you point them out, even if the flaws are not actually there. Stand up, square your shoulders, and say instead, "Here is my best."

CHAPTER FOUR

THE GENESIS OF A LEADER

A man's worth is no greater than his ambitions.

MARCUS AURELIUS, ROMAN EMPEROR (121-180)

F rustrated by my job's lack of creative potential and little promise of a career path ahead, I was driven to find an exciting new opportunity. Instead of working in a government bureaucracy, I wanted the freedom to create and expand and grow. I found it at a nonprofit organization, Answers in Genesis (AiG).

AiG publishes magazines and books, produces films, and funds research that provides evidence of God's existence and runs an internationally recognized museum in Kentucky.

As a trained graphic artist, I could see that a great artist created this world with purpose and style. When I look at the stars on a dark night or enjoy the crash of the ocean's wave on the shore, I find artistic beauty, not accidental combustion. When I marvel at a fine wine, I see a master vintner. I do not believe our universe and our lives are the result of cosmic coincidence or a proverbial toss of the dice but rather that life and the world around us are the special creations of an intelligent, all-knowing designer. I believe it is our responsibility to learn about and take care of His planet. AiG espoused a thought process that was more mandolin and less wolf, and I loved it.

I went to AiG's website one afternoon to just browse. Their publications looked great, but the website was very basic and lacked a special polish. So, I e-mailed them: "To whom it may concern: I'm a graphic artist and I'm interested in working for you." The general manager contacted me and asked when I could visit the company for an interview.

I told him I'd be there on Monday. I was immediately offered a job. I put in my two-weeks notice at the extension service, put my house up for rent, and moved my young family—Jan was expecting our second child, Adam—to a place, oddly enough, not far from the second American home of my great-grandfather Luigi!

My job at AiG offered so many more creative opportunities than I'd had working for the state, and I was having a great time. My design work was in full color on coated paper, instead of in black and white on matte paper. I was cranking out projects left and right: book covers, VHS cases, posters, CD/cassette-tape covers for music, and kids' music.

Less than a year went by before my employer said, "Brandon, we want you to take over the website. If you want to hire people and build up our site, that would be great." That was music to my ears! I hired a programmer, a content manager, and even got an intern. The four of us together built AiG's website from a little brochure page to a deep site, rich with content. Now, of course, it's massive.

Quickly realizing that we needed to constantly refresh the content on our site if we wanted return visitors, I came up with a model for publishing new posts on the website, daily. I would recycle already-published magazine content because the company generated a lot of original material that was always relevant.

We were diligent about keeping the content fresh because we wanted our followers to be engaged. Every day, there was a reason to visit the site, and our audience started to respond. Web traffic started pouring in, especially when we initiated an e-mail newsletter guiding them to the website.

If you don't put out something new every single day, you're going to lose your audience because there won't be a reason for them to check in. Every day you lose a pair of eyes is a day you have made an impact, a difference, a sale. Money never sleeps. If you're not getting in front of your audience regularly, you'll find they will direct their attention to your competitors.

I also ran the online store, and once we got visitors regularly coming back to the site day after day, we were able to put our products in front of them too. These experiences and what I learned became a model for my own company, Liberty Alliance.

As we started seeing this exponential expansion of sales, thanks to a dynamic website, people inside and outside the organization began to take notice. I was invited to a business meeting with a publicly traded company located in San Francisco. It was a wonderful experience for a kid who had grown up in rural West Virginia. We got to see the Golden Gate Bridge and ate at amazing Italian restaurants. I was flying high with exuberance.

I was eager to share that kind of experience with everyone at the company and to commend my staff for their great work. I set up a digital kiosk over the web department with a scrolling marquee screen where we'd highlight the traffic numbers for the website. The numbers would scroll across the screen: "This month's traffic numbers: one million. This month's sales: $50,000."

Remember that at this point in my life, I was still very young, and I was pretty idealistic. I was proud and happy to see how successfully we were getting the company message out to the big World Wide Web, and I was so relieved to be out of the government system where I'd felt stifled. Our little web team was celebrating successes out loud, something that I came to understand is very important in every business. All I wanted to do was to share that feeling with everyone and inspire us all to achieve even more.

Sometimes, people judge your motives. Sometimes, their negative opinion is deserved, and sometimes, it isn't. Sometimes, you'll understand where you could have done something differently to avoid the negative outcome. But you can't let that wolf of criticism discourage you.

AiG's president, Ken Ham, and our board of directors treated me as though I were a prodigy. They raised my salary, gave me a company car, and invited me to every board meeting—before I was even an executive. I was just a new, upstart, middle-management guy, but soon I was traveling to semi-annual board meetings and sitting with all the directors and executive team, who presented me as "our web guru, Brandon. Wait until you hear his report."

They were proud of what I had accomplished and of everything I was doing for the company. It was intoxicating and spurred me to work even harder and do more. To other department heads it was probably seen as unbridled ambition, brown-nosing, or a combination of the two.

After a few years of hard work, I was promoted to the position of executive vice president. I was an eager twenty-nine-year old kid running a multimillion-dollar nonprofit company and overseeing some of the same people who had hired and trained me. In retrospect, it's no wonder I could count my friends around the water cooler on one hand. This really ate at me, so I vowed I would focus on making others successful along with myself.

Looking back, I realize I was compelled to succeed. Would I be where I am today if I hadn't been so ambitious? Perhaps not, though it can get lonely when you're galloping full-speed ahead.

One time, I remember Ken pulling me into his office to tell me I was "a wild stallion. You remind me of me." He was an exacting leader with extremely high standards. It's no exaggeration to say that he expected perfection, and he didn't tolerate laziness or mistakes. He wanted the best out of each team member. As I moved up in leadership, I was put in charge of firing people who couldn't measure up. I had to let a lot of people go, and I began to hate being "that guy." Though I was not yet aware of it, my calling would be found in building and inspiring, not solely in management and administrative necessities.

I think I resented having to let people go over what seemed to be less-than-significant infractions. But now, after years of owning my own business, I better understand Ken's thinking, and I've come to respect his standards. I've also come to learn that it's not just the company that can suffer when someone needs to be fired. Other team members may be forced to pick up the slack or be put out by obvious incompetence or disrespect. Troublesome employees may need a wake-up call that forces them to seek a position that offers more chance of success. Holding on to an employee you know isn't cutting it is toxic to everyone involved.

Ken Ham is also a brilliant marketer and communicator. His Australian accent makes him fascinating to listen to, and millions of people all over the world have done so with rapt attention, for decades. We would run an event and pull in $100,000 in product sales over a weekend, and that was because he was an incredible salesman. From his lectern he could mention things that people would line up to buy, afterward. I learned a lot from watching him work. He would bundle products in the most ingenious way. He'd say to the crowd, "People ask me what one book I would recommend. I recommend these three." And people would rush out the doors to the tables and buy all three.

The most important thing I learned from working for Ken Ham was the power of a mailing list, knowledge that I used to great effect years later to build my *Inc.* 5000 company, Liberty Alliance.

Put bluntly, a good mailing list is a money-making machine. AiG worked with millions of dollars by raising donations and selling products through a massive mailing list. As Ken traveled around the country, he passed around a clipboard at every event to collect the names and addresses of his audience members. Eventually, we added a line for an e-mail address when e-mail became more common. He would come back to the office and hand it to the office staff, who would manually key in every single address and e-mail address. By the time they hired me, AiG had been in existence for about four years and already had over one hundred thousand people on its mailing list.

That may not sound like a lot of people in the grand scheme of things, but when those one hundred thousand people had heard Ken speak and were supercharged over what he was talking about and had taken the time to put their name and address on a clipboard, they thereafter faithfully read every piece of literature that came in their mailbox from us.

Engagement was through the roof because people knew that while they were signing up for the newsletter, they would also get a monthly fundraising letter. And when Ken sent a fundraising letter, chances were high that a large percentage of recipients were going to return the envelope to us with a check and a pledge for a future donation. When he sent a newsletter with a mini-catalog of products, a good percentage of the recipients bought the products.

I remember marveling at the power an organization can have. Within a few days of sending out a letter, money would start pouring in. I began campaigns to increase the size of the e-mail list, and we began conducting e-mail fundraising as well. My web team set up a way to receive donations online so that we could get access to funds instantly. We didn't have postage or printing expenses. We just sent out an e-mail with a link to the online store and rapidly watched the donations pour into the bank account within forty-eight hours. That was revolutionary.

It was while I was still at AiG that I started a business venture with my dad, one close to our hearts. Dad and I both love history and we happened to discover that the first version of the Bible brought to America by the Pilgrims in 1620 had gone out of print not long after that period.

A little over four hundred years later, my Dad and I had this version of the 1599 Geneva Bible restored page by page in order to republish it in a modern edition. It's still, word for word, the same as the original, which is part of its charm, so it reads as if it were in Middle English, but all of the spellings, punctuation, and font have been updated for readability.

We borrowed money to get started, and three years later, we went to print, rolling those Bibles off the presses for the first time in four hundred years. Since then, we've distributed over one hundred thousand copies of the 1599 Geneva Bible. If you'd like to know more, visit GenevaBible.com where its popularity is still strong.

At this point I had a full-time job, a side project, and three young children. That probably was enough to keep me busy, but I'd always wanted to earn my master's degree by the time I was thirty years old. I also wanted to gain more credibility at AiG. I had read somewhere that people who have an MBA make more money than those who don't, so that was enough encouragement for me to pursue the degree.

The executive track MBA at Thomas More College, which was taught at night school, was my choice, given my full-time day job. Because my salary at the nonprofit was not enough to pay for my studies, I took out a student loan. The cost, plus the hours it took to complete the work, made it quite a challenge. But I got a lot out of it.

I would recommend to anyone considering studying for an MBA to not to get it right out of college. Go and work somewhere for a few years and gain some experience. I found it much easier to apply the book knowledge I was receiving after having already gained valuable hands-on experience in management.

Working full time with three small children while earning an MBA did make for a long day, though. I was up very early, getting ready, checking e-mails. I arrived at the office by 7:30 a.m., and put in a full, hard day of work, not leaving the office until 6:00 or 7:00 p.m. most days. But my work didn't stop even then. E-mails piled up and the phone rang well into the night.

On two nights a week, I would leave the office and go straight to night school. Classes went from 6:00 until 10:00 p.m., and we had a study group for another four hours on a second night of the week.

For the rest of the week, we had research, writing, and projects to prepare.

As AiG's EVP, I'd often get phone calls that couldn't wait until I was out of class, so sometimes, I had to step out. Ken might be on the West Coast with a problem. Though only 6:00 p.m. out there, it was 9:00 p.m. on the East Coast, but it didn't matter what time it was, the problem still had to be dealt with despite the hour.

Honestly, I didn't mind the challenges. I thrived on defeating the wolves. I was the only person in the class who was a second in command, and one of the few who had to provide for young kids and a wife at home.

You won't find me saying it wasn't difficult to juggle it all, but I learned to stick with it even when it seemed impossible. It's largely why I found myself actively seeking out the mandolin moments in life. They don't just happen. You have to make the effort to find the time to sit and enjoy a glass of wine. You don't gulp it down and dash out the door. You can't smoke a good cigar quickly. You must savor it and enjoy the moments you're celebrating.

At the end of my MBA program, I had to choose a company to research for my thesis work. I chose AiG, which had several offices around the world at that time in Canada, Great Britain, Japan, New Zealand, and Australia.

I spent a few weeks at the Australian office interviewing the leadership there. They had a very different management philosophy than our US office did. I wanted to implement some of their suggestions, which I believed could really benefit the US office. My findings and recommendations, however, ended up creating some friction among the management at the US office and, eventually, led to my resignation.

It was at about this point that I became aware of American Vision (AV), a nonprofit organization in Georgia. I liked this company because its message was that we could change the world for the better in every area of life. AV promoted the utopian vision that we could make a difference—and should. It was our God-given duty to outsmart the wolves and enjoy the mandolin. You know me by now. That vision fired me up, and I wanted to be a part of it!

A week before I was hired at AV, I got a little ahead of myself and submitted a letter to the board of directors at AiG listing my concerns and my hope that changes could be made that would benefit the company. As you might imagine, it did not have the positive impact I had hoped for, and instead, I learned a very valuable lesson: how you say it is as important as what you say.

My employment at AiG came to a sudden and jarring end. I had just enough in my bank account to get us through the next few weeks while I waited for AV's decision regarding my employment. I had a moment of fear that my candidacy for the AV position could be jeopardized by the manner in which my employment had just ended at AiG.

But, thankfully, my new boss, Gary, and the board at AV saw past all that and presented me with the opportunity to take what I had learned up to that point and apply it to my burgeoning career. Our move from Kentucky to Georgia held the promise of new beginnings.

What I Know to Be True

I believe God is the great artistic creator. What good is that knowledge if I don't do anything with it? I've always believed it's our responsibility to do what we can to improve on the great world that's been given to us. We can make it better, economically. We can create more freedom and prosperity and encourage more peace and moments of calm despite the wolves of stress, demanding bosses, and long, hard days.

Especially when we are young, our tendency is to gallop ahead, plowing over others who might be on the same path we are. We must learn that the mandolin might only be heard if we make the effort to stop and listen. And by doing so ourselves, we may encourage others to join us in enjoying the privileges of life.

CHAPTER FIVE

A VISION FOR AMERICA

Where there is no vision, the people perish.

PROVERBS 29:18

When I first moved to Georgia in 2004, my dad and I climbed Cobb County's Kennesaw Mountain, which boasts a lot of Civil War-era history. At this 1,808-foot elevation, you can see Atlanta's skyline very clearly. On the opposite side, a ridge of mountains in Paulding County is visible. I would later find my current home there.

Just a few miles away sprawls the town where the drama represented by Fess Parker and Jeffrey Hunter in the 1950s movie *The Great Locomotive Chase* unfolded during the Civil War. In 1862 The General locomotive was stolen by Union spies at Big Shanty station—now historic, downtown Kennesaw—and ran a few miles north before being recaptured by the Confederates. The author Joel Chandler Harris characterized the event as "the boldest adventure of the war."

I had just made my boldest career adventure with my move down to Georgia. As my dad and I took in that sweeping view, we had a premonition of the future and made the comment that "one day, the Vallorani name will have made an impression on this landscape. We'll have put down roots here. We'll have spread our family legacy across the state of Georgia."

At that point, I had a small house and was still working for someone else, making a nonprofit salary. I had only touched on the research of my family history and had no idea of the impact the legends of my ancestors would have on my future brand, Vallorani Estates. Over the next twelve years, I would lay the foundations to realize that vision.

Before I made the decision to work at AV, I had mentioned the idea to a fundraising consultant at AiG. His question was, "How big are they?" I said, "Well, their budget is half a million dollars a year."

He just looked at me, aghast. I was heading from a nonprofit with a budget of twelve to fifteen million dollars to one with an annual budget of half a million dollars. "That's crazy. Don't do it. It's career suicide. Why would you even consider that? You should be looking to go to an even bigger nonprofit, not a smaller one." And he wasn't the only one who thought so.

But what I saw was the opportunity to take what I had learned and apply it to a smaller nonprofit in order to make that organization grow to it's full potential. The consultant meant well, but he mistook me for an administrator. At this point, I was just beginning to understand that I am an entrepreneur, a risk-taking builder, not a caution-centric maintainer.

Starting and growing companies is what I love, and it works for me. I got to guide AiG's Internet division from nothing to something big. Now I was given the chance to help AV grow by 600 percent over three years.

Yes, AV was smaller, but getting to employ the techniques I had learned and developed at AiG helped us boost AV's annual revenue from a few hundred thousand dollars to several million in a few short years.

Seeing AV's exploding growth was intoxicating, and I loved the opportunity to work for Gary DeMar and AV in particular because we promoted the philosophy that we could and should change the world into a better place. That message really attracted me because I'm an idealistic person who wants to enjoy the privileges of life and help others enjoy them with me. We should always strive to make ourselves and our world a better place. AV provided its constituents the resources and information to do just that.

From radio programming and events to graphic design and e-mail marketing, I took everything I had learned up to this point and applied it to AV. We had to hire a full-time team of customer-service and warehouse personnel to handle the influx of orders we were receiving. One of our interns was responsible for putting all of our radio recordings online. We started running out of materials and couldn't get them reprinted fast enough. We had to create a better web platform to handle all of the content and traffic, moving everything from the old system to the new one.

But I'd learned more than how to build up a business; I had learned some big lessons on how to garner excellence from my employees through inspiration, as my father had always done, rather than through coercion or fear. I had learned that I needed to be more sensitive to the people around me. It wasn't all about the end goals of the business. It was about the people I was organizing and whose abilities I was harnessing, which would make all of this good stuff happen.

In hindsight, I should have spent more time applauding each and every employee at AiG for what that individual had done, as opposed to being the lone wolf going to board meetings where I got all the glory. I don't think I mistreated employees, but I didn't treat them the way I'd like to treat them now. Ideally, what I want and love to hear is, "Hey, I *want* to work for Brandon!"

It's amazing what happens when you start giving credit to your employees for the success of your company, how inspired they are to continue that success, and what a positive atmosphere it creates. As Ronald Reagan said, "There is no limit to the amount of good you can do if you don't care who gets the credit." Now that I really understand how important it is to give others credit, I enjoy praising my team's work: "Look at what so-and-so has done in the marketing department. Look at what so-and-so has done in the web department. They're doing a great job." People will see the success you foster, and your reward for that success will be found in a happy, positive, and self-driven workforce.

Another big takeaway from my experience is the importance of moving fast in marketing. When I had an idea, I would roll with it immediately. Two hours later, if the response wasn't meeting my expectations, I'd tweak it, perhaps repackage the item with something else, and advertise it again.

Especially today, digital marketing has changed the game so drastically that the ability to tweak quickly is an absolute necessity. For example, when you are paying per impression with Facebook and Google ads, you don't want to waste your entire marketing budget if an ad is getting views but not engaging the clicks that can translate into revenue.

The trick is being willing and able to turn on a dime rather than waiting around for results. Ultimately, it didn't matter if I'd spent four hours creating an ad. If it wasn't working, I would pull it and do something different. This approach has enabled me to sell more than

$25 million in products online during my career. And once something worked, I didn't stop with a single run! If something works once, find success with it again . . . and again if it works a third time!

Recently, I decided to codify the successful approach I'd learned and retool it as the five tips for selling products that will work in nearly any business. Here they are:

Brandon's Five Tips for Selling Any Product

1. *Make it irresistible.* Why does the customer need this product? You've felt that urge. But it doesn't matter how good your product is if you don't deliver on the basic need your product will fill—be it ease, comfort, or survival. People won't buy it if they don't see a need for it. Establishing that need starts with creating the story around the product, the story that engages the reader or listener and makes it impossible to resist the urge that they must have it.

2. *Establish the value.* By now, prospective customers want this thing you're selling, but do they want it more than the money in their pocket? You need to convince them that the product is worth more to them than it costs, that it's a good trade of money for product. Businesspeople often make the mistake of thinking they have to set a certain price here because they need a certain margin. But your margins don't matter if you don't sell your goods. If the customer does not want to pay that price, you're not going to sell anything and your margins are irrelevant. You have

---

to convince prospects that their hard-earned money is not worth as much as your amazing product is to them.

3. *Set a limitation.* You have to set a limitation of some kind, whether that's limiting the quantity available or putting a time stamp on the price point. For example, "Only one hundred left in stock!" or "This price is only available for twenty-four hours!" Then, if it is an e-mail campaign, you send prospects reminder e-mails warning of even greater scarcity: "Only twenty-seven left in stock!" Otherwise, they're likely to decide to get to it later and, in the end, forget about it altogether. They may decide that, after all, they can live without it. You must create the sense of urgency that demands immediate action. E-mail advertising is much more effective than print advertising for this step and one reason my business has seen great success. Buy now!

4. *Make an unbelievable offer.* To channel *The Godfather*, you've got to make your customers an offer they can't refuse. You've seen the television commercials selling some amazing gadget to make your life better. You're already sold on it. It's a terrific product, and the price is good. They've established that you have to call now because the price is going to rise, or they're going to run out of these great gadgets. But what do they all do to push you over the edge and call that 1-800 number immediately? The announcer adds, "But wait! We're going to give you a second gadget absolutely free." That is that extra little bump that I call the unbelievable factor. It's too good to be true. It has my warehouse manager freaking out because I've already

got a killer ad, and now I'm going to make it a buy-one-get-one-free offer. "My gosh, we can't do that! We won't make any money! We'll run out. This offer is too good!" You know you've got a killer ad when your inventory manager is freaking out. Sure, you've got smaller margins by throwing in an extra unit or giving free shipping. But you'll make more money overall due to a much higher volume sold! Plus you're reaching more people with your products and getting more people on your e-mail list. They're sharing it with their friends because it's such an amazing deal. You've got ambassadors running around promoting your brand and your products. Is it risky? Yes. Welcome to the world of the entrepreneur. You can't make it big if you aren't willing to risk it big.

5. *Build a big mailing list.* Do you want to build your e-mail/mailing list fast? Here's a great tip: give something away. Totally free. We once ran a campaign at American Vision for a completely free audio CD. All you had to do was ask for it. Yes, the production and shipping cost to send out those CDs was several thousand dollars, and now I was just giving it away. What was I thinking? That audio CD got people interested in American Vision and all that we had to offer. Essentially, it was an advertisement cloaked as a free product. We tracked future sales that came in from the people who received that CD, and the residual revenue was in the hundreds of thousands of dollars, far outweighing the costs. Notice how this tip combines all of the first four tips? It's a shortcut, but you must be willing to give something away.

I once had an employee who would walk into my office a little peeved to tell me, "Well, we sold out of this (item) again." That's kind of the point, right? I would hear it all the time: "You're selling them too fast. Now we're going to need to reprint them." Well, that's great! Now we can advertise: "Back in print due to popular demand. Have you ordered your copy yet? Order before we run out!"

I'd get pushback, sometimes, from staff thinking we ought to raise our prices. Someone who hasn't had experience in marketing might say, "You need to raise your price if it's selling this fast," and I'd have to explain there's no magic that works like that. Believe me, if it did, I'd just double or triple my prices. But gouging the market doesn't work, not long term, anyway.

The market will tell you what you can sell your product for. My team has learned to find the sweet spot on each product. We learned the maximum a customer would pay for particular items. If we had gone above that product price, we'd have wound up with a full warehouse and an empty bank account. Margins are irrelevant if prospects aren't interested in trading their cash for your product.

Offering free shipping is a great example of adding value that will make your warehouse and accountants nervous. Customers look at shipping as a "nothing" that they're paying for. Of course, many customers understand that they're saving time and money by not having to drive to a store, search for that item, and stand in a checkout line, but not everyone sees that value. In my experience, many online customers view shipping costs as a tax. They push a button and get taxed to have that product appear on their doorstep a few days later.

What we've found is that raising our item price slightly and giving free shipping will actually make it sell better than if we were to lower the price of the item and charge for shipping.

We built a mailing list and an e-mail list at AV that was much larger than the organization had previously had. We built a brand-new website that featured new articles every day, something not done in the past. E-mail newsletters featuring the new content drove our web traffic up.

Next came a better online store that used e-mail to drive sales higher and to increase the revenue coming into the organization. Our radio network grew to broadcasting on twenty-five stations. The publishing department exploded under my direction, going from one or two books released each year to a dozen new books per year. It was an exciting time, reminiscent of the pioneer days of steel and coal that my great-grandfather Luigi experienced. It seemed there was no end to the growth spurts.

One particular book took AV to a whole new level. Ironically, it was also the success of this book that gave me the momentum to become fully self-employed.

What I Know to Be True

You cannot burn bridges. Even when things aren't going the way I would like or staff aren't living up to my expectations or situations are getting out of hand, I don't let myself stoop down to the level of a growling, snarling animal. You must always be the bigger person, and this philosophy has been instrumental in the building of my companies. Ignore the wolves. Focus instead on what I call a mandolin moment.

As Zig Ziglar said, "When you encourage others, you in the process are encouraged because you're making a com-

mitment and a difference in that person's life."[2] Encouragement really does make a difference. I've learned time and again that encouraging, inspiring, and motivating my staff works far better in the long run than fear-based management.

When I was the sword hand of an exacting boss, I was in the habit of meting out swift judgment. But when I attempt to run my businesses in that manner, it never works well for me, because that's not who I am. I'm an encourager, an inspirer, and that approach has served me very well. It's important to me to help people enjoy life's privileges rather than be fearful of a life without them.

2 "Zig Ziglar Quotes," BrainyQuote, https://www.brainyquote.com/quotes/quotes/z/zigziglar617776.html.

CHAPTER SIX

THE TIPPING POINT

The tipping point is that magic moment when an idea, trend, or social behavior crosses a threshold, tips, and spreads like wildfire.

MALCOLM GLADWELL, AUTHOR

I t was a dusty old book that was my tipping point, *The Christian Life and Character of the Civil Institutions of the United States*, a thousand-page book published in 1864. What a title, right? This was, essentially, a historic encyclopedia made up of letters, quotes, essays, and other writings that underlined the Christian character of the founding of the United States. Drawing from multiple historical sources, it showed that counter to what the ACLU, among others, claims, this country was indeed founded by people who had a Christian ideal in mind.

In a climate in which secularists were looking to strip inscriptions such as "In God We Trust" from our money, take prayer out of schools, ban statues of the Ten Commandments, and further secularize the country, this book was exactly what the religious right needed to prove that, yes, we were conceived and intended to thrive as a Christian nation.

Gary, the president of AV, quoted the book in a radio debate on the subject of religious liberty with an ACLU attorney. The ACLU attorney was audibly nervous and upset about this book. "Where is this book? I've never heard about this book. I want to know about this." It was as if Gary had just revealed a secret weapon.

When Gary told her it was out of print, she was relieved. "Oh good. It's out of print. It's not a problem." Gary's immediate response was, "We'll fix that. We've got to put it back in print." We took that story and used it to create the need for the book. We ended up using a headline that read, "The ACLU's Worst Nightmare."

When I arrived at AV in 2004, the organization was filling, perhaps, forty orders a week. When the book *The Christian Life and Character of the Civil Institutions of the United States* came out with that big-ad push and marketing efforts, it exploded into more like forty orders an hour. Following my five tips for selling any product, AV sold a million dollars' worth of the book in one year. Let me tell you how we did it and why it helped me launch my own business.

We started out selling that book to AV's own mailing list. That's when an opportunity presented itself that would change the way we did business from then on. And it is what later launched my realization that I could make enough money selling products to start my own business.

Our small nonprofit had arranged a national conference for our constituents in 2007. Our team was on its way out the door to North Carolina to staff this conference. A few hours before I was supposed to be on the road, I got a phone call from a salesman for Newsmax. com, the biggest player in those days. "Hey, Brandon, due to a cancellation, I've got an e-mail advertising slot available that's going to be seen by eight hundred thousand people. It's $8,000 if you want it." I remember looking over at Gary's son, James, who was our intern at the time, and saying, "What do you think? This ad that we've already created using the five tips for selling has been proven successful through our own mailing list. We've already sold more than any other resource."

At that point we were working with a much smaller mailing list, maybe one hundred thousand names. "How about if we take that same ad and ran it to eight hundred thousand people? Does the math work?"

We did the math and decided, "Yes, it works." It was a risk, no doubt about it. What if it fell flat and I had just put our payroll money on the line? Remember that in the nonprofit world every dollar you have is even more precious than in the for-profit world! But the math worked, so I gave the salesman the company credit-card number over the phone, and we jumped in the car and drove to North Carolina.

When I got to our conference location, I mentioned my decision to Gary. He was flabbergasted, especially because I'd gone ahead without running it by him first. I remember he held up his clamshell cell phone, pointed to it, and said, "That's what these things are for."

At that point, for that company, $8,000 was a huge amount. But by the time we started setting up our laptops at the event, e-mails were already flooding in from this ad.

We sold $40,000 worth of books in one day. That ad paid for itself four times over. We couldn't even stay at the event we'd organized. Half of us had to go back home because the minimal staff back at the office couldn't handle all the orders coming in. Believe me. It was an exciting problem to have. Gary was still shaking his head at me. He kept saying, "I can't believe you spent $8,000 on an ad." All I could say was, "But we made $40,000." He forgave me, eventually. We're even business partners now.

Something in my gut told me that if a small list of one hundred thousand e-mails could do well with this product, it was worth the money and effort to send it out to a much bigger list despite the risk. Ultimately, this example is one reason why I believe that it's sometimes better to ask for forgiveness than permission. But you have to be willing to face the consequences whichever way the dice fall.

There were many business lessons packed into that one experience of renting that e-mail list. For starters, everything I'd learned up to this point was proven. All the pieces were in place: an inspired staff; a massive mailing list; an incredible product with a great story, at a great price, and in a limited quantity; and we threw in free shipping to make it an offer prospective customers couldn't refuse. Liz and Ashley, our customer-service representatives at that time, couldn't keep up with all the phone calls and e-mails. The entire web, radio, and customer-service staff had to drop everything and help the warehouse ship all the books out several times. We could hardly keep up with the demand.

Something clicked in my mind at that point. I knew I was ready to go off on my own. If I could achieve this success for other companies, why not for my own?

In 2008, just as my success at AV began to pay off, the banking collapse sent the economy spiraling downward. Our donations all but vanished, as did our sales. As a nonprofit we had to retrench and tighten our belts. I offered to take a $10,000 salary cut, and Gary took one too.

It was going to be tough. I had five kids now. Thankfully, my Bible publishing company, Tolle Lege Press, brought in a little extra income each month. But I had a premonition that AV had reached its zenith. If I wanted to continue to grow my income and create a new world of possibility, I needed to strike out into unchartered territory, this time completely on my own.

Just as my great-grandfather Luigi had, I needed to put my family first and do whatever it took to take care of them. As with every major decision I made, this decision was made during a convergence of factors.

I took the pay cut to help the company, despite the personal stress. The good news was that I had already seen what e-mail marketing and a big mailing list could do. Simultaneously, I was broadening my marketing strategies beyond the limitations of the Christian right to a wider-ranging, more mainstream Republican market. I was leaving the nonprofit world behind me and heading full-speed into capitalism.

Lastly, I knew in my heart that I could be successful on my own, and frankly, I was weary of justifying my decisions to those in authority over me. Though I was the executive vice president and had a lot of authority, I still answered to the president and the board members every six months on financial matters and operations. They'd tell me what they thought I needed to do, and while that was helpful, I felt I was already putting enough pressure on myself to perform. It wasn't always as simple as it sounded.

It was time to face the wolf of risk and step out on my own. All I needed was the right product. It was late in 2007. The presidential election was coming up in 2008. It seemed at that point that the Democratic nominee was going to be Hillary Clinton.

An exposé film titled *Hillary Uncensored* came across my desk, and I wanted to market that DVD. But I knew I could not do so through AV. As a 501(c)3 organization, AV was not legally allowed to involve itself in politics in such an outright manner. We would have been liable to lose our tax exemption if we had promoted or assailed specific candidates or legislation.

It was my opportunity! I told Gary I wanted to sell the DVD on my own, outside the nonprofit. He told me to go for it.

I'd never been anything less than upfront with Gary, and I would never have considered going behind his back with this idea. Much of my success with my own entrepreneurial endeavors has been because I have sought to do business with integrity. Gary's attitude of support and encouragement without hesitation when I told him I wanted to branch out on my own and sell the DVD was terrific. He's one of those people who is happy for others to succeed.

It was time. Now ready to take the risk of climbing out of the tree, I found my way down the path on my own, with a product that wouldn't compete with AV.

What I Know to Be True

An entrepreneur's life is a series of death and resurrection experiences. Jobs and products die, and new and better ones take their place. We should not be afraid of wolves masquerading as change or risk. I hit my ceiling at WVU and left for AiG.

I hit my ceiling at AiG and left for AV. Now I had hit my ceiling at AV. What was about to happen next was a risk. I could fall flat in my attempts to build my own business, or perhaps, my future would be even bigger and more exciting than I had imagined.

It was because I was willing to take that risk that I now enjoy the freedom created by owning my own business. I am able to focus on developing my brand, Vallorani

Estates, into a household name as I help others join me in enjoying the privileges of life and provide for my family well above basic needs.

CHAPTER SEVEN

AN ENTREPRENEUR'S DREAM

If you're going to be thinking, you may as well think big.

Donald Trump

I

n order to sell *Hillary Uncensored*, I needed to form a legitimate business. I have a vivid memory of December 7, 2007, when I walked into the courthouse in Dallas, Georgia, to get my business license. That same day I opened up a bank account, created an online store, established my merchant account to take payments, and uploaded the product information to begin selling that DVD.

I moved quickly. I had to! Money never sleeps, and every day I waited to get started was another day my growing family would feel the sting of my pay cut! Taking good care of my family motivated me to succeed, just as taking care of his family had driven Luigi.

For two reasons, I named my business Discount Book Distributors. First, I didn't want to limit myself to any particular ideology. This name sounded official and unaffiliated. Second, I had discovered that I could get sharply discounted backlisted and discontinued books from publishers for pennies on the dollar.

For $2,500, I could buy ten thousand books the publishers found difficult to sell for whatever reason. The title might not have been catchy, or the marketing copy might have been subpar. Whatever the case, I planned to craft and send an eye-catching e-mail advertisement to a mailing list I had rented using my five tips for selling any product. I would establish a need for this title, listing the full retail price to demonstrate value, and offering a discount for a limited period: "But wait! The price has been slashed for a limited time. Order your copy now before it is out of print and you can't find it anywhere."

Though I might only sell the books for $5 or $10 each, I was still making a lot of profit and building my own e-mail list with every purchase. That was the first major business that I started, with the same idea I had brought from AiG to AV: transitioning from making a modest impact with a small mailing list within a small organization to making a big impact with a large mailing list promoting a broad array of products.

I attribute much of this big-picture thinking to my mother and father's encouragement, inspiration, and insistence that I do my best during my formative years. Okay wasn't good enough. Enough wasn't enough! I could do more. So I did.

My business, at that time, was run out of my basement office. My garage was the warehouse. I created and marketed products each evening, and my wife, Jan, would pack and ship the orders in between homeschooling the kids. I remember looking at my bank account one day and seeing that over $40,000 had amassed. Wow. It used to take me eight months to make that much money!

Then the 2008 election season heated up. It was looking as though Hillary was going to be eclipsed by Barrack Obama. Hillary's radical leftist agenda concerned me, and while I loved the idea of Americans electing minority candidates, I found Obama's socialist politics even more detrimental to the freedom our forefathers had fought so hard to gain and had crafted so carefully for the generations to follow.

Have you ever had a moment when you realized you had to try to do something, anything, if it meant preserving something for future generations? Every time we take a family portrait or save some heirloom for a child or grandchild, we are taking action to ensure what is important to us is passed down to our descendants. I knew I had to take action to try and preserve our conservative values for generations to come, like Luigi had sought to do by sending Eugene back to America. In just such a moment I had a radical idea: *I wonder if my mailing list would want a "NObama" bumper sticker.*

That night I designed the sticker and crafted the e-mail ad. Once again, I walked through the door labeled "risk" and decided to give the sticker away, completely free, to anyone who wanted it. All I asked for was a nominal fee to cover a portion of the shipping costs. Of course, their e-mail address would now be a part of my growing mailing list.

Entrepreneurs don't always have venture capital before they start, or angel investors as we so often hear of in miracle stories published in business magazines. My family was surviving on my recently cut salary, but my fledgling business could only grow if I had money to rent e-mail lists and buy product in order to use that revenue to swing to the next product and next e-mail-list rental.

Swiping a personal credit card for this latest ad to give away a sticker—a moment rife with risks—left me pacing the floor waiting for my ad to be sent to the e-mail list I had rented. The wolves of doubt started to crowd around me. I fled to the highest branches of optimism in my mind and waited.

The ad was sent.

Ding. An order.

Ding. Another order. Ding ding. Ding! Ding! Ding!

Orders started pouring in faster than my wife and I could process them. One night I went to bed and woke up a few hours later to several thousand orders. Customers began to get upset as we struggled to keep up with the demand. The risks I took paid off in a big way, as many do. The Olympic wrestler and head coach Dan Gable said, "If you're afraid to fail, you'll never succeed."[3] How true I have found this to be.

I'll admit, I'm also an opportunist. I guess I get that from Luigi too. After experiencing this kind of success, I thought I could make a living in the political world. If an opportunity vine presents itself outside your wheelhouse, grab it and swing to the next opportunity vine. Staying in your comfort zone can be less stressful and possibly require a lot less effort, but it often limits your ability to grow and succeed. Don't be afraid to latch on to a new idea or completely change your entire corporate mind-set if it could mean improvement.

It was time to rebrand because I had determined to become exclusively political, and I needed a politically oriented store, not a site that sounded like a book club. I rebranded the name of Discount Book Distributors as PatriotDepot.com, which still does very well. Today over one and a half million dollars in retail sales and thousands of orders pour in annually for our resources, which range from T-shirts and bumper stickers to novelty items to philosophical books and educational DVDs.

PatriotDepot.com quickly became a critical force in propelling the Tea Party movement to the forefront of media attention. Starting in 2007, I had begun to build the infrastructure that would allow us to be a massive force in the conservative political arena, and we did so

---

3 "Dan Gable," inspiringquotes, http://www.inspiringquotes.us/quotes/TuSf_S82o0lU1.

with such success that we have been recognized as a key player even by those associated with the left side of the aisle.

Cars bearing our numerous bumper stickers appeared all across the country. We started having meetings with people who would become media giants in the political world. One such person we were privileged to give a donation to went on to create the Tea Party Patriots, a well-known grassroots watchdog movement.

We're the ones who determined to deliver over one million tea bags to Washington, DC, in 2009, a nod to Boston's biggest moment in history. By working with Reagan.org, we obtained a permit to conduct a peaceful protest by delivering the tea bags to an area near the White House. The truck was being unloaded at our chosen spot when NPS agents stated the permit we had obtained was not the "correct" one, technically a violation of our First Amendment rights.

Congress shall make no law respecting an establishment of religion or prohibiting the free exercise thereof; or abridging the freedom of speech, or of the press; or the right of the people peaceably to assemble, and to petition the government for the redress of grievances.

We were told to remove the boxes of tea bags. Rather than admit defeat, we coordinated with another local Tea Party-friendly group that allowed us to place the tea bags on its private property. Bumping into wolves along the way can't stop you from getting home. You simply have to figure out a way to survive the moment. Even this story has a lesson that reminds us to never accept no as an answer.

Many people vilify the Tea Party, accusing it of things that have nothing to do with the truth about the movement, which was first, last, and always about unfair taxation. I was proud we were part of bringing the message of fiscal responsibility to a government that seemed to have forgotten just whose money it was they spent so freely.

THE WOLVES & THE MANDOLIN

I was coming up with new stuff every day, trying to keep up with demand. We were selling "Don't Tread on Me" flags, and "Come and Take It" caps. Every political phrase you can imagine we printed on T-shirts and bumper stickers. The more Obama talked about big-government policy, the more followers—and sales—we made. It was fun!

I'd get an idea for a bumper sticker in the morning, design it myself (my graphic-design background really came in handy), and put the product online by the afternoon. I wrote the advertisement and sent out the e-mail blast myself—simple as that. I created a machine that just got bigger and bigger and bigger, but it also got hungrier and hungrier and hungrier. I had to keep feeding it. The monster was growing, and now I was getting to the point where the tail was wagging the dog.

We always needed more customers, more products, and new places to advertise. My staff was growing to meet the demands, and I now was responsible for their livelihoods. Management and executive leadership is not just a fun job in which calling all the shots gives you a big salary.

What so many don't understand is that CEOs and other executives get those big salaries because they have so many hard decisions to make and a huge amount of responsibility on their shoulders.

> Congress shall make no law respecting an establishment of religion or prohibiting the free exercise thereof; or abridging the freedom of speech, or of the press; or the right of the people peaceably to assemble, and to petition the government for the redress of grievances.

92

For example, my brother-in-law Kenny left a successful career in another state to become my business manager. His loyalty and attention to every detail drives me to succeed even more. It's not just about my family being taken care of now. I am also responsible for the families of every single person on my team. If I fail, they fail.

Frankly, at a certain point, purely online retail became exhausting, even with the success I was enjoying. By the time I paid for products, advertising, and labor, the margins were too thin. Something had to give to keep us growing, and I didn't want to be just a peddler of goods for the rest of my career.

One day, I was reconciling my bank statements and noticed Google had sent me $100. I couldn't for the life of me understand why I got $100 from Google. I went down the hall to my web developer, Jonathan, and said, "Hey, what is this money for?" He told me, "You have some Google ads running on one of your websites, and they finally paid you because you hit $100 in earnings."

I scoured my various websites and found where AdSense was set up. I said, "Do you mean to tell me people come to a page and click ads and I get paid?" I was scouring my various websites to find where Google AdSense was set up. He said, "Yes, you even get paid a little just from people seeing the ad." Another vine of opportunity drifted in front of me, so I reached out and quickly grabbed it.

Building on what I had learned, I started up a news website, PatriotUpdate.com, where we posted news articles every day. We started sending newsletters with snippets of these articles to our mailing list every day, and hundreds of thousands of visitors started flocking to the site.

We hired qualified writers to produce original content and aggregated news from other reputable news sources. We considered ourselves Drudge on steroids. Our subscribers read a preliminary paragraph in the email newsletter, and click to "Read the rest of the story." That click sends them to our website, where they read the article, and they see and, possibly, click on the ads. We get paid. Immediately, the advertising revenue from Google started pouring in. That created two revenue streams in my business—and advertising has much higher margins than retail sales.

Keep in mind that I was continually working to build my mailing list because that was what allowed us, effectively, to print more money, which, in turn, allowed us to grow even further. We were constantly renting other e-mail lists like Newsmax, Townhall, Human Events, and GOPUSA, and we always offered something free, such as my first bumper-sticker ad that launched the entire company: "Free bumper sticker. Just pay shipping and handling!"—literally in minutes, I'd have ten thousand orders. The shipping-and-handling costs basically paid my expenses for printing and mailing, so I wasn't making money there, but I was growing my mailing list.

During this time, I worked with a terrific guy who is a list broker. He helped me find lists to rent. One day I asked Steve, "Can you rent out my list?" At that point, I had about eighty thousand unique e-mail addresses. He said, "Get it to one hundred thousand, and I'll rent your list."

That was a powerful incentive for me. We tripled our efforts and finally got to one hundred thousand names. I said, "Okay, Steve, here's my list. Rent it." So he got in touch with his customers, brokered the deals, and wired me the proceeds, which were just ridiculous amounts of money—$20,000 a week. I started making more money in a month than I used to make in a year.

Now I had three revenue streams: retail, advertising, and allowing political candidates and organizations to rent my e-mail list. I realized

I was making some good money on one site, and I wondered whether creating another website would mirror this success.

We created another website and another e-mail list, and again, the same thing. So now we had three streams of revenue coming in from two sites. Then we did it again. We replicated this strategy three or four times, and the business grew exponentially.

We could hardly keep up. It was a good challenge to have but a challenge nonetheless. As many entrepreneurs will tell you, when you are bursting with success you can often encounter a pack of wolves.

Suddenly, you find yourself hiring anyone you can because you need help so badly. You might give in to the habit of throwing money or resources at a problem rather than finding a long-term solution because it seems more advantageous in the moment. Staff start to complain they're overworked. Because you can't imagine finding the time to deal with recruiting and training someone new, you throw a raise at an employee who might be happier elsewhere. Your expenses and administrative headaches are growing just as quickly as your profits.

One piece of advice I want to pass on is to hire slowly and fire quickly. You'll find much less drama—and trauma—if you make an effort to do this.

I can honestly say today that while I thrive on the building phase, with the growing-things phase, I've sometimes found it best to move a little more slowly. It's important to consult others before charging ahead—for example, discussing with colleagues whether to take on a new project or not.

After having replicated the business model about four times, I realized I'd maxed out how many times I could do this successfully. Now I was meeting with more and more people in the conservative movement. They were very interesting people with unique messages but little to no platform. They included learned people who were writing books and articles and who were speakers or news giants. They were not necessarily businessmen, marketers, or web designers but, rather, content providers. They needed the infrastructure I had created to build revenue so they could continue getting their content out to the public. Basically, they needed a back-office team that could generate revenue, and I had everything in place to provide it for them.

One of those people was Victoria Jackson, a *Saturday Night Live* cast member who became a Tea Party spokesperson. She's a dynamo entertainer and a smart and persuasive conservative voice. But without the background structure of television producers and promoters, her message might not reach the world at large. I said, "Hey, Vicky, how about we start a website together? And I will do the same thing for your website that I'm doing for mine."

We started an Internet TV show and *The Victoria Jackson Show* website. I had a small studio where we produced episodes. One of the guests on her show was a guy named Doug Giles. As I watched Doug talk to Victoria Jackson, I realized the guy was awesome.

After explaining what I was doing, he agreed to partner with me to launch a site, Clash Daily. Since it was our first project outside of our company, I offered to split revenue fifty fifty. We shook hands on the deal and built a successful and profitable business from the ground up. Doug and I are still partners—and friends—today.

It became apparent that I needed a brand that tied all of my websites and partner websites together. PatriotDepot.com and PatriotUpdate.com were thriving, and now I was realizing I could coordinate a network of other politically minded personalities. I wanted to leverage the power we could have if we were all on the same team, harnessed to the same vision. It would be an alliance of kings and queens, not just individual personalities trying to make it alone.

Thus Liberty Alliance emerged. I purchased the domain LibertyAlliance.com for $2,000 and used economies of scale to build on what I was already doing to increase the margins so that we were all making more money and reaching more people with every passing week. Our network continued to grow.

We started inviting partners such as Joe Wurzelbacher (a.k.a. Joe the Plumber) who became a conservative-folk hero after a viral video. He is now our VP of partner relations and a great addition to our team. We partnered with actor Kirk Cameron, who starred in *Growing Pains* and now has a thriving marriage and family-enrichment platform, and with Colonel Allen West, a conservative politician and pundit from Florida often featured on *Fox News* and other political programs. We've partnered with *Fox News* and Newsmax TV personalities and countless writers and speakers across the country— even some freedom lovers in other countries!

These are great partnerships for all of us because these brilliant people provide their engaging content and commentary for the public, and we provide monetization and the back-office infrastructure of ad placement, vendor relationships, accounting, even product fulfillment where applicable.

The partnership mentality I instituted from the beginning means all parties bring something equally valuable to the table. In the business world, it might more closely resemble a client-vendor relationship, but I see it as a partnership because it is a win-win for both parties, and we rely on each other to have an impact. We provide our services at no upfront cost to the content providers, and in return, our efforts are paid for through the revenue we create for them. Everyone wins. It's my favorite way to conduct business!

Liberty Alliance mushroomed in 2012, and as of 2016, we've been listed on the *Inc.* 5000 List of America's Fastest-Growing Companies for five years in a row, a privilege not every business can claim. We have generated over $50 million in revenue since our inception in 2007. We are very proud of the success we have experienced for ourselves and for our partners.

During the first few years, I was the designer and the marketer, and I even handled product shipments at one point, a regular one-man band. I began hiring people to do web development and accounting, but I still did the marketing and product creation for a long time. By 2012 I was acting as the CEO and had a full staff to manage operations, including an executive assistant to handle my evermore complicated schedule and travel arrangements.

It was a dream come true for me. I felt invincible. We all did. We bought a printing company to print our own bumper stickers and T-shirts and renamed it Liberty Printing. One idea always led to another, and that's how I got into the firearms business and started Liberty Guns.

I had one employee who had a real spark about him. He was very enthusiastic, a go-getter, eager to do well, eager to be whatever we needed. We hired Scott to handle e-marketing for PatriotDepot. com, and about three months in, we realized this guy knew everything about guns. He was practically a two-legged encyclopedia of firearms knowledge.

We decided that since he was already handling product sales well and knew guns, and our market loved guns, we should get into that business and start a firearm-sales division. So I got my federal firearms license and expanded into selling licensed firearms and ammo and accessories.

It would have been easy for us to tell ourselves that firearms were not what we did or that Scott hadn't been hired to sell firearms. Instead, we changed Scott's role entirely. He became the VP and general manager of a successful division because he knew something we didn't know and put his heart and soul into that passion, on the clock and off the clock.

Tragically, Scott was killed in an automobile accident on his way home from work in August 2015, something none of us will ever fully recover from. I'd never lost an employee like that before. It hit all of us very hard. Scott Johnston was one of the best I had ever had working for me. In the hours preceding his accident, as he was closing up the store, I saw him vacuuming the front area. That is real leadership and humility in action. I will never forget that. Rest in peace, brother.

The year 2015 was very difficult for me. Early that year, our gun store was burglarized through the neighboring unit that was undergoing construction, and $20,000 worth of firearms was stolen in a few minutes. That was definitely a big, bad, ugly wolf. Thankfully, the Bureau of Alcohol, Tobacco, and Firearms (ATF) investigators ruled there wasn't much we could have done differently to avoid the incident, but it was a sucker punch to the gut. Then Scott was killed a few months later. The wolves were closing in.

On the night of Scott's accident, I was in discussions with a competitor who was considering a buyout of Liberty Alliance for several million dollars, but the deal didn't go through at the last minute, and I was disappointed.

I had found myself at the top of an empire that, while successful, encountered cash-flow and operational challenges often, and my administrative attention was required constantly—remember I am a builder, not a maintainer.

I was already developing my next new entrepreneurial interests, including Vallorani Estates, and I was forced to continue giving time and administrative attention to Liberty Alliance in order to keep it flying upward. Everything needed my attention now more than ever. Juggling a dozen spinning plates at all times while successfully balancing on a see-saw became not only a hope but a requirement to keep all the wolves at bay.

My brother Jared now acts as Liberty Alliance's CEO, and my son Adam (still in high school) works in the advertising department as an intern. Having the ability to give my family members a career path is extremely satisfying, and I can work on developing the Vallorani Estates brand.

By the end of 2015 I had been self-employed for eight years, and I had faced many wolves. I had begun to realize I couldn't wait for the mandolin moments to come to me—I had to pursue them, find them, and take the time to enjoy them. It became evident that my next and biggest goal was to help others find and enjoy those moments and find a way to face their own wolves.

What I Know to Be True

It's always easier to stay within the comfort zone of what you've done before, but that's not how you grow. Those who see openings where others see a brick wall are the ones who make history. And don't get so wrapped up in the task at hand that you stop looking at the world around you for opportunities, because they pop up when and where you least expect them.

Everything you do or learn or try may not succeed in and of itself. In fact, you're going to fail occasionally if you're really trying, but failure can lead you to something new you'd not have otherwise considered or maybe even been aware of. Keep moving, keep learning, and keep seeking out like-minded people and exchanging ideas with them.

CHAPTER EIGHT

FACING YOUR WOLVES

Fear is a reaction. Courage is a decision.

Sir Winston S. Churchill

I n April 2014 Doug Giles and I, along with my boys, went to southern Florida on what I thought would be a routine hunting trip. Doug is an avid hunter, having bagged big game all over the planet. We'd already been on several exciting rifle hunts together, bringing down water buffalo, black buck antelope, Père David's deer, and wild boar.

Little did I know, however, that this time I would come face-to-face with a wild boar and the only thing that would keep his razor-sharp teeth from entering my body was a six-inch knife.

Sometimes, too, they'd eat a newborn calf if the mama cow couldn't keep them horned away. Or a baby fawn that the doe had left hidden in the tall grass. Once, in a real dry time, Papa and I saw an old sow standing belly deep in a drying up pothole of water, catching and eating perch that were trapped in there and couldn't get away.

THE WOLVES & THE MANDOLIN

Most of these meat eaters were old hogs, however. Starvation, during some bad drought or extra cold winter, had forced them to eat anything they could get hold of. Papa said they generally started out by feeding on the carcass of some deer or cow that had died, then going from there to catching and killing live meat. He told a tale about how one old range hog had caught him when he was a baby and his folks got there just barely in time to save him.

It was that sort of thing, I guess, that always made Mama so afraid of wild hogs. The least little old biting shoat could make her take cover. She didn't like it a bit when I started out to catch and mark all the pigs that our sows had raised that year. She knew we had it to do, else we couldn't tell our hogs from those of the neighbors. But she didn't like the idea of my doing it alone.

"But I'm not working hop alone, Mama," I pointed out. "I've got Old Yeller, and Burn Sanderson says he's a real good hog dog."

"That doesn't mean a thing," Mama said. "All hog dogs are good ones. A good one is the only kind that can work hogs and live. But the best dog in the world won't keep you from getting cut all to pieces if you ever make a slip."

Well, Mama was right. I'd worked with Papa enough to know that any time you messed with a wild hog, you were asking for trouble. Let him alone, and he'll generally snort and run from you on sight, the same as a deer. But once you corner him, he's the most dangerous animal that ever lived in Texas. Catch a squealing pig out of the bunch, and you've got a battle on your hands. All of them will turn on you at one time and here they'll come, roaring and popping their teeth, cutting high and fast with gleaming white tushes that they keep whetted to the sharpness of knife points. And there's no bluff to them, either. They mean business. They'll kill you if they can get to you; and if you're not fast footed and don't keep a close watch, they'll get to you.[4]

It all started the night before as Doug and I drank vodka and smoked cigars around the glowing campfire. The guides were telling us stories of their dangerous and exotic hunts. The boys and I were riveted to our seats, eyes wide, hearts pounding, when Doug and his daughter Regis told me that I had not truly hunted until I had faced an angry boar with the end of a spear. They challenged me to an epic battle of man versus monster the next day.

I will admit I was a little afraid at first. I had heard many stories of people who were maimed or even killed by wild-boar attacks. Feral boars are a serious concern. Considered pests, they overrun the wild areas and wreak havoc on neighborhoods, threatening hikers and small children. In 2014 a squirrel hunter in Louisiana encountered a boar that ripped his legs apart and caused significant loss of blood.

When threatened, boars will either run away or come at you like a freight train. One never knows until it's too late. Death on four feet, these mythical beasts often attack their victims on the inside of the leg, with their tusks, severing the femoral artery, and the victims bleed out with one quick slash. We've likely all seen and/or read *Old Yeller!*

By the end of the evening, they had talked me into it. I thought of Luigi being a "pretty tough guy" and tried to gather my courage.

---

4 Fred Gipson, *Old Yeller* (1956).

That night I tossed and turned in my bed. I went through several mental exercises of how I would spear this hog and pin him to the ground. I had no choice but to beat him.

The next morning, I woke early to the sound of hunting dogs howling with anticipation. These dogs love to chase hogs. They literally live for it. You can learn a lot from these dogs, many of which sustain injuries doing what they love.

Doug and I lit up our cigars, climbed in the swamp buggies, and went out into the palmetto jungle in search of wild hogs with the guides and dogs. My heart was pounding. I kept wiping my sweaty palms on my jeans. The cigar and the fresh morning air as we drove a while began to calm my nerves.

Things stayed relatively quiet until the chase dog caught wind of a wild boar. He flung himself off the truck and disappeared into the thick brush. It wasn't long before I heard the barking replaced by the squeals of a very angry hog.

The chase dog runs after the hog and wears him down. At this point the guides release the catch dog, which bites down on the hog's head and holds him until the hunter can get in close enough for the kill. Before we jumped off the swamp buggy and headed to face the dog-captured hog, I reached for the spear. It wasn't there. I asked Doug to help me find it. That's when he said, "Forget the spear. Use this knife."

What? Are you kidding? I had mentally rehearsed going on this hunt with a long heavy spear I wielded from a safe distance, not getting up close and personal with a dangerous hog and a mere six-inch knife!

There was no time to argue. I followed the guides through the brush. It was so thick you could only see about two feet in front of you. Doug was behind me with a rifle in the event things got nasty.

106

The sound of squeals, growls, and thrashing was getting louder and louder.

As I rounded a palmetto bush, I saw a feral hog that was as big as a black bear. The catch dog was growing fatigued and the hog was starting to flip him around like a rag doll. My adrenaline and testosterone kicked into high gear. It was either me or the hog, and I wasn't going to die today. What good were Luigi's legendary stories of near-death escapes if I fell to a wild pig?

So, without any more hesitation, I took the blade and sank it deep into the angry beast, just behind the shoulder. I stabbed him a couple more times to be sure because he kept thrashing in anger, trying to get at me. The hot blood ran down my hands as the massive hog breathed his last. I had done it! I shook from the adrenaline rush for several minutes afterward.

After the hunt, the full impact of what had happened began to sink in. I had faced one of life's biggest, baddest "wolves" and beaten it. Not only had man won over wild beast, but we were able to donate the meat from that hog to feed the children of the Seminole Indian Reservation. I don't believe in wasting anything I've hunted. My family or other people's families have all been fed from what I've hunted.

This hog hunt quickly became a metaphor for the rest of my life. I know now that I can overcome fear with courage. I can face the wolves, sometimes climbing a tree to avoid them, playing the mandolin until they are calmed so I can continue on my way. It helps me to know I can fight the wild beasts that surround me in business and in life and still enjoy the music of life.

Three Kinds of Wolves You Might Face

The world is hell-bent on separating you from your money and your time. People are very happy to take both from you. They're like wolves in that respect. You must be sharply aware of these wolves and do what you can to avoid them. Helping people in need is not what I refer to here, as I advocate and regularly give to a number of causes and charities.

No, I refer to those who will nickel-and-dime your business until you realize your pockets are empty. They'll expense the three-mile trip to the store to pick up a cable for their office. They'll arrive ten minutes late and leave five minutes early. They'll charge a personal purchase to a company card.

Money is money, and time is also money. There are those who ask for an unscheduled minute and take twenty unscheduled minutes. Dan Kennedy aptly named them time vampires. When you're a busy executive or entrepreneur, you are juggling so much at all times that every minute in your day is your lifeblood, and unscheduled interruptions are wolves. Don't let time and money wolves bleed you dry.

The other thing I've learned is that the world loves to tell you no: No, you cannot do that. No, you cannot have this loan. No, you will not be able to achieve that. No, you must do it our way instead. No, no, no, no. I hate being told no. When I set my mind on something, I will get it. When I get it, I sometimes realize I really didn't want it, but I got it anyway because they told me no. Don't let the "no" wolves deter you from walking your path. Find a way around the no.

FINANCIAL WOLVES

I've always been a "go-big-or-go-home" kind of guy, and I have encouraged everyone who has worked for me to pursue growth. That has worked. We grew really, really quickly, but there are challenges with growing so quickly. We were staffing up too quickly and too heavily partly because I love creating jobs and giving people opportunities and partly because it could often be more propitious to throw another staff member into a department rather than solve and resolve the broken system that person was being tossed into.

At one time, we had over fifty-five employees on staff and it was a little out of hand. Even though the revenue was pouring in, we sometimes found ourselves struggling to make payroll. My empire had gone from a fast-paced think tank that ran efficiently with a lean staff to a bloated kingdom of processes and meetings. It could take four hours to get through some of our staff meetings because we had so many departments and projects.

When I told one of my business mentors about the financial wolves I was facing from growing so quickly and not having the cash flow to fund the next phase of growth, he pointed out that my business, while profitable, was consuming profits for breakfast so nothing was left for lunch and dinner. A major capital infusion would provide a phenomenal boost to my business, keeping our growth trending strongly upward.

Though we've always been very profitable, and though our growth rose at a rate of 67 percent over the three-year period from 2013 to 2015, getting cash from lenders for a business like mine is very difficult. Traditional banks don't always understand an Internet-based business model. They ask, "Where's your store?" "Well, it's online." "Then how do you get people to buy stuff?" "We send them an e-mail." "Well, but . . . how are you maintaining a sustainable model long term?"

It doesn't really suffice that we've been doing it successfully for years, as have millions of other Internet tycoons of our modern era. Banks need their risks to be covered with collateral, and they don't even know what to list as collateral if it's all digital: e-mail lists, Facebook followers, online stores, digital downloads, and clickable ad spots instead of buildings, inventory, and other physical assets that banks traditionally recognize.

Even venture capitalists have a hard time with our version of business because they're looking for new ideas, new untried products and services. We're not really selling a new idea. They're looking for some innovative technology that nobody else has, but that isn't what we do.

What I have is a business model that has worked time over time and has, subsequently, been imitated by a lot of my competitors. In fact, during the 2016 election cycle, the *New York Times* called Liberty Alliance a company that "found a way to create something sustainable and even potentially transformational . . . Liberty's countless news-oriented pages . . . have become an almost ubiquitous presence on right-leaning politics on Facebook in the last few years."[5] Some have called Liberty Alliance one of the most powerful conglomerates in the conservative arena today.

Two or three times, we looked into applying for a Small Business Administration (SBA) loan, but the process is a nightmare for anyone with little spare time. It involves a three-inch stack of paperwork,

5 John Herrman, "Inside Facebook's (Totally Insane, Unintentionally Gigantic, Hyperpartisan) Political-Media Machine," *The New York Times Magazine*, August 24, 2016, http://www.nytimes.com/2016/08/28/magazine/inside-facebooks-totally-insane-unintentionally-gigantic-hyperpartisan-political-media-machine.html.

with demands on format, required projections, budgets and analysis, executive bios, and estimated growth plans. It's a full-time job applying for an SBA loan. Every time we'd begin, we'd quickly look at the hours the process would demand, shrug, and say, "We simply don't have the time to stop making money in order to work through the SBA's loan requirements. We're making it somehow. Let's just keep going."

I was eventually able to get a small bank loan for $60,000 in 2011. By then, we were bringing in $60,000 in a week in revenue, so we hardly felt its benefits. Now we are bringing in revenue of more than $10,000,000 per year, all without a big bank loan or groups of investors. It's been boot-strapped the whole way. December 7, 2017, will be the tenth anniversary of my break into entrepreneurial pursuits with that first political DVD.

So how have I fended off this ever-present financial wolf? I've used my personal credit.

When push comes to shove, I use my personal credit to fund my business. It's not uncommon among entrepreneurs. The man who started Tito's Vodka funded his start-up using a wallet full of personal credit cards because he believed in his product so firmly. So did the founder of CheapOAir. And the big one: Google. In 1996 two PhD students worked on their research paper out of their dorm rooms at Stanford University. Two years later, they spread the costs of starting their search-engine company over three personal credit cards.

And yes, it can be scary to put your credit on the line, to possibly risk digging yourself a massive hole of debt to fall into, but you've got to make it happen. If you believe in something and you know what you're doing can be successful, you just do it and kind of figure out the details as you go along.

Especially at the beginning, I had to use my personal credit often, but I couldn't worry about not being able to pay it off. I didn't have an investor or funding. The only way my start-up was going to be successful was to fund it myself.

I would use that fistful of credit cards as a line of credit: charge them up, pay them down, charge 'em up, and pay them down. I didn't realize the havoc this would wreak with my credit rating until I decided I wanted to buy a camping trailer for my family.

The RV dealer had the perfect camper for $17,000. I wanted it. A good-ol'-boy financier was sitting behind the desk. He asked me how much money I made. His response to my reply was positive, clearly a sure sign I'd be approved for the loan. Then he ran my credit, and his face fell. "I'm real sorry, son, but we're not going to be able to finance you."

My mouth fell open. "What are you talking about? I make a lot of money. I've always paid my bills on time. What's the problem?"

"I'm real sorry, son. We just can't do it."

There was no way I was walking out of there without that camper, not when I had been working my tail off to provide for my family's needs. It was time for a want to be fulfilled, and I wanted that camper! I checked my bank account balance on my phone. "How about I write you a check for the full amount?" Man, he sat back in his chair and said, "Well, all right, then. We'll take a personal check!"

That was a wake-up call for me that I needed to get the business expenses off my personal credit. It was time to take my banking to a business level, separate from my personal accounts.

When I realized something I was doing was hurting my credit score, I subscribed to one of the free credit-report services, and I started monitoring it and learning everything I could about the system. I had a dozen credit cards with balances ranging from

$10,000 to $25,000 that the business was constantly maxing out, paying off, and maxing out again.

Thinking I was avoiding interest, I paid the balance in full but then charged it again, so credit reporting always showed a revolving balance that never diminished. Though I was paying my credit-card balances off each month, credit reports showed only that I was paying on time. It didn't show that the balance was paid in full or only partially paid; it merely showed I paid. When you carry a balance over the reporting date, you look as if you're always owing that amount and not able to pay your balance off, which drives your score down because your debt-to-available-credit ratio has to be a certain percentage.

From that point on, I didn't want to let the banks tell me no. I have learned when the credit report is scheduled for each of my cards, and I take serious measures to ensure none of my cards have a high balance on them on that date. My credit score has soared since then, and I have learned to manage it and keep it high so I can always borrow money for my business and personal needs.

People used to believe cash is king, but the real truth is that cash flow is king because as long as you have cash funneling into your business and you have time to put that cash to work before a bill becomes due, you're good, but when the cash flow dries up, you're dead.

If I'm selling products and I'm making some money but not much, that money is moving into my world. I get to hold on to it and put it to work for a couple of weeks before it goes back out again, and that time can be vital for a small business. I have to play a sort of shuffling game in which I use the credit card to run the ad, and by the time I have to pay the credit-card bill, I'll have made the money back on the sales from the ad. But if I run the credit card for the ad and don't sell the product—perhaps because I didn't follow my five tips for selling any product—then I won't have the money to pay the bill when it becomes due. A lack of cash flow is like a whole pack of wolves that surround you quickly.

ADMINISTRATIVE WOLVES

Individually, administrative problems aren't that scary, but collectively, they pack together like wolves snapping at an entrepreneur's heels. They threaten to drain money, time, energy, and happiness.

1. Keeping Inventory Turning

As soon as you invest in inventory, you're making the decision to lock up your cash. The only way to get that cash back is to sell the product—hopefully, for more than the price you paid. But you sometimes have to cut your losses and sell your products at a lower margin to have cash coming in and not just inventory sitting there.

Let's say you paid two dollars for a particular product, and you want to sell it for five. You've run the ad for five, but you only got a handful of orders. Now the product's just sitting there on the shelf, not selling for anything. It's better to sell it at cost for two dollars and turn it back into cash that you can use again on a better idea than it is to tell yourself that if you sell it for two dollars you won't make any money. It doesn't make any difference. It's sitting on your shelf, making nothing. It's tying up the money you have in it. Liquidate it. Get that money and put it back in your business and give it a chance to grow through something else.

2. Touch It Once

Don't put an item on a to-do list if you can get it done right away. Here's an example. Ideas often hit me when I'm at a staff meeting, listening to reports, one-by-one. Sometimes, I write ideas down and come back to them after I have had time to consider them. However, if I know an idea is a great one, I immediately send an e-mail or a text to the people I want on the project. I save time by not revisiting the issue later, and e-mailing/texting gets the ball rolling faster. Remember money never sleeps. Every day—every hour—lost is time you could have realized a greater success.

3. Management by Walking Around (MBWA)

I'm a big believer in MBWA. I have had as few as three and as many as fifty-five employees, all in different divisions that I just pop into casually say, "Hey. How's it going? What are you working on?" Their words might trigger something in my mind that I heard from somebody down the hall who's working on a different project. That's how you get collaboration going, find new ideas, and solve problems.

I may find someone processing a video when I walk in, and I'll ask him what's going on. He may tell me the process has been taking a while because his computer's slow—it's three years old. Here I am, paying this guy a big salary to produce product I can sell, but he's got an aging computer that's wasting hours of his productivity and delaying our sales. All he needs is a new computer.

Those are the kind of things you'll never learn just by sitting behind a desk or in a project report meeting. The employee might never ask for a new computer, and you might never know he could be more productive if his computer were upgraded. You have to get up and walk around and talk to your employees on their turf. MBWA is one way to discover and fix inefficiencies as well as come up with winning ideas.

4. Make Your Meetings Matter

We used to have individual departmental meetings, but when we transitioned to weekly meetings where all departments came together, the camaraderie improved. Everyone knew everybody and began to see the big picture and to understand what each colleague was working on. And then ideas start to popcorn around. "Hey. I'm doing this. How might that work with what you're doing?" I firmly believe in the importance of getting all the staff in one room on a routine basis every week. We went to monthly meetings for a while, but it was just too much to discuss, and the meetings got too lengthy. I have business associates who conduct shorter daily huddles. Regardless of how long your all-staff meetings are or how often you hold them, they create an opportunity for everyone in the room to talk, toss around ideas, get to understand each other, and know each other's project list.

There's been a backlash against meetings in the corporate world, with people groaning over "death by meetings," and yes, it can certainly happen. But meetings also play a vital role because they foster collaboration and camaraderie.

At our meetings, I let everybody talk; it's not just me handing down the word from on high. We're not terribly structured. There is a little time for cutting up and enjoying a good laugh, but there's also opportunity for everyone to hear what his or her fellow employees are working on and what the next phase is going to be. Somebody across the table might piggyback off something, and there's a lot of give and take. Yet it does take discipline to ensure the meetings don't run haphazardly, wasting hours of collective time.

On the one hand, if we present the agenda and request that everyone stick to it and we tell people when their scheduled time is up, everybody feels stifled and unable to provide input. The opposite is a free-for-all in which multiple conversations are taking place simultaneously and doodling is the most productive takeaway. Both of those extremes are unhelpful. Somewhere in the middle is the best. A good meeting should have an exchange of ideas, a general flow, and be calmly disciplined but also engaging.

THE "NO" WOLVES

Winston Churchill once said never, never, never, give up. Books, mantras, movies, and even songs urge us to believe and achieve. The sentiment almost garners an eye roll in today's cynical world.

Life is full of obstacles, and there are people who will tell you no. It's one of the first words we hear as a child—often to protect us from danger. We learn to say it, especially as parents, almost without thinking.

As we get older, we must learn to graduate from no to yes. In business, we know to adhere to the no of not breaking laws or of being unethical. But the majority of the world is bent on saying no to you, to which most people will say okay and change their course around the wolf standing in the path, baring its teeth with a warning growl.

I often tell my team to never take no for an answer. It is when you figure out the way around a seemingly insurmountable problem, a harsh rejection, or a potential failure that you learn what true success feels like. Every problem has a solution. Brick walls can be climbed, chipped away, or driven straight through. Even the largest boar can be brought down with a small blade. Wolves can be calmed by the sound of the mandolin.

When my fifth child was a baby, I was invited to Cancun on a business trip with a group of other executives. The deal was to bring my wife to Cancun, stay in a really swanky hotel, and inspire each other over cocktails. I was really looking forward to it, obviously! So was my wife.

I got to the airport in Atlanta with my wife and my six-week-old baby girl, who was too young to leave behind. We'd arranged a sitter for the other kids. We were all set to fly first class to Cancun and go on this exotic trip. It was going to be wonderful. My wife was excited. I was excited. Then the ticket agent asked to see the baby's passport.

We looked at each other in shock. I had completely overlooked that the baby would need a passport to travel. My wife's face fell. "I'm just going to take the baby and go home. You can go without me." She was crying.

I said, "Oh, no you're not. We're going to go on this trip. I am going to find a way to go on this trip." I asked the ticket agent if I could use a birth certificate.

She looked as if she felt sorry for me but said no.

I said, "How long does it take to get a passport? Can I get a passport today?"

"It takes a long time, but there is a place that does rush passports and can turn them around in a week." This trip was an opportunity that wouldn't wait a week for a passport!

I told Jan, "You are not going home. You just stay right here with the baby." I got on the phone with the State Department and learned there are only five cities in the USA where you can get a same-day passport: Atlanta, Los Angeles, New York, Chicago, and Houston. Obviously, I tried Atlanta first, but Atlanta appointments were booked for days in advance. Then I thought, *Well, heck, Houston is on the way to Cancun.* Sure enough, I got an appointment for 9:00 a.m. the next day in Houston to get a same-day passport.

We redirected our flight to stop in Houston. With just hours to spare before departure—again—we raced home and got all the

CHAPTER EIGHT: FACING YOUR WOLVES

materials: birth certificate, photos—everything. We got to Houston just in time for our twenty-minute slot, and I got my little girl a same-day passport. We were all on the next flight to Cancun and only missed one day of that special trip.

I remember my business partner saying, "Lesser men would have caved and let the wife go home." But that's not me. There was no freaking way we were going to miss that trip. I could have gone by myself, I guess, but it honestly never occurred to me that leaving my wife behind would be an acceptable outcome.

You can't let a brick wall stop you. You must figure out a way around it. Don't let the "no" wolves stop you from continuing down the path to the next village.

Mandolin Moments

Life is more than just outsmarting wolves. My great-uncle spent the majority of his time bringing joy to many people as he played his mandolin throughout the Apennine villages of Abruzzo. As your business, wealth, and influence grows, you have a responsibility to share the privileges of life with others.

Success breeds success. As I became more and more successful, I began noticing more and more successful, interesting people were joining my circle. Spending time around those interesting people often resulted in our creating a new business idea together. Also, now that I have the ability to afford it, I've been able to travel the world, and as a result, I've enjoyed some great countries and cultures. We've taken exotic cruises, and I've been able to give my executives those experiences too because I believe that treating people well comes back to you in more ways than you can imagine, and I've seen that play out time and time again.

Whether you call it karma or God's blessing, I do believe that doing well by your colleagues, partners, staff, and fellow men will come back to you, many times over. That's also how I've forged amazing working relationships with some of the celebrities I've collaborated with. I don't want to be the guy with my hand out. I never, ever ask them for money. We make a deal, and they get the checks as we split the profits.

What's the point of making a lot of money and having a lot of success in life if you're not sharing it with the world around you? It's this very thought that came to mind when I first considered creating the Vallorani Estates brand.

I was enjoying the best cigar I'd ever had. At hand sat palatial perfection in the form of an imported Italian wine from Colli del Tronto's Vigneti Vallorani, and I could smell freshly roasted coffee from where I sat, looking out over the same landscape I had once viewed from the top of Kennesaw Mountain.

How can I hoard these mandolin moments? How can I hold back for myself the enjoyment of life's privileges? It was then that I knew my next entrepreneurial endeavor would be about helping the world around me savor the mandolin moments, not just outsmart the wolves.

LEAD PEOPLE

Don't manage human resources. I absolutely abhor the term *human resources*. People are not human resources. They are human beings with families and dreams. It is my hope that one of the big contributions to my success has been how I lead people. For the most part, my leadership philosophy came naturally but also incrementally. Through my experiences, I would see what worked and didn't work.

A few years ago, my COO, Liz, suggested that our executive team read *The Orange Revolution*. I highly recommend this book. It solidifies what I had come to realize over my years in management: You will get much further with a carrot in front than a stick behind. You will get more from your employees by inspiring them to achieve the company mission than you will by making them afraid of what will happen if they mess up.

Always have something ahead that's good. Always provide encouragement and incentive. Always have a goal you want the team to achieve. But at the same time, as is well-known, you can't get lazy or inattentive without consequence.

When I'm true to myself, I'm a better leader. Not that I can't learn from other people, but intuitively, I read people well and just follow my instincts, which I think are in my DNA from my dad.

To me it's the difference between being a boss or a leader. A boss tells you what to do and how to do it and checks to make sure you are doing it. A leader inspires you to do your best and accomplish his vision in your own unique way, and he trusts while he verifies.

My brother Jared once told me, "Tell us what hill to take and we will take it." Your team should be ready to take any hill for you because they're inspired by what you're trying to achieve and not because they're terrified of the consequences they'll face if they fail. You'll also find that they'll be less likely to fail if they're inspired instead of hounded!

When someone isn't performing at the level I hope for, I always start the conversation with a list of what they're doing right. When I get to the part where I need to confront their deficiency, I preface my comments by saying, "Look. Your greatest strength is also a weakness. I like how this particular trait yields these results, but here's where it can cause a problem. Let's address the problem and figure out a solution." Then I end with, "But overall I'm very pleased." Creating a sandwich of concern with positive affirmations and praise on either side comes across as less of a personal attack and more of a guide to increased success.

On occasion, middle management will tell me, "So-and-so needs to be fired." I resist acting on an impulse until I've made absolutely sure that, as a leader, I've done everything I can to make that person successful. Sometimes, the employee is moved to another department. I coach the employee. I have a "sit-down" to outline what will help to achieve success because when an employee is successful, we all win.

When I do fire employees, it's the absolute last resort because I put most of the blame on myself if they didn't achieve success within my company. I want them to succeed! I hired them because I believed in their potential. Generally, when I have to let people go, I have exhausted every means of reaching them, inspiring them, and getting them fully on board. If all this fails to produce the required results, there's no other option but to end the professional relationship.

Keeping people who are not productive damages the morale of the whole team. It also prevents them from doing something they are really good at and enjoy doing. Don't keep them out of the market while they limp along in your company for so long that they cannot find successful employment elsewhere.

ENJOY THE GOOD LIFE

I like traveling to cool places. Nothing quite invigorates the creativity and inspiration required to operate and build businesses as much as the sights, sounds, and smells of a different culture. I also like to dress well, and I've noticed that the better I dress, the higher the level of service I enjoy. People simply respond to you differently when you look polished and classy.

The Italians actually have a phrase for it, *la bella figura*, which translates to "cutting a beautiful figure." They believe, as do I, that taking pride in how you present yourself to the world changes how the world sees you. There's a reason many of the top fashion icons of our day are Italian, no?

Everything in life is about marketing. When you dress to present yourself well, you are marketing yourself as someone who cares about the details, who knows how to look good, and who should be listened to. Presenting yourself well also can increase your self-confidence.

The more I experienced this kind of heightened level of living—the exotic travel, the successful people I was meeting, the pleasures of the good life—the more I wanted to use my business knowledge for something more in tune with my personal philosophies. I wanted to take a break from fighting wolves, to play the mandolin until dawn.

It was this new thinking that would eventually bring me back, full circle, to my Italian heritage. In 2016 I determined to create my lifestyle brand, Vallorani Estates, to share the mandolin moments with the world at large.

My goal is to reach the many determined, successful professionals—or those who aspire to be such. These individuals are busy, tired, and, possibly, overworked executives and entrepreneurs who want . . . need . . . to take a break from fighting the various wolves on their life's path in order to enjoy the music of the mandolin.

What I Know to Be True

Risk is essential for success. Among the many things I've learned is how and when to take a risk. Consider what

will happen if your plan fails and decide if you're prepared for the consequences. But also weigh the rewards. Go with your gut. Risk is a four-letter word to some people, but for me, accepting risk has been a real game changer and has rewarded me time over time.

The harder and smarter you work, the more opportunities will present themselves. Don't just take every opportunity. Look for the most promising and then move—and move quickly.

Don't accept no as an answer. If a bank says no, try another bank. If all banks say no, ask friends for capital to get you through. I've done this many times, and I have built an incredible amount of trust because I never, ever fail to pay a debt. I also commit to a pleasant interest to sweeten their sacrifice.

"Never give in, never give in, never, never, never, never—in nothing, great or small, large or petty—never give in except to convictions of honour and good sense. Never yield to force; never yield to the apparently overwhelming might of the enemy. We stood all alone a year ago, and to many countries it seemed that our account was closed, we were finished. All this tradition of ours, our songs, our School history, this part of the history of this country, were gone and finished and liquidated."[6]
—Winston Churchill

---

6 "Winston Churchill, "Never Give In" (Harrow School, London, England, October, 29, 1941).

CHAPTER NINE

COMING HOME: VALLORANI ESTATES

*When you rise in the morning, think of what precious privilege
it is to be alive, to breathe, to think, to enjoy, to love.*

MARCUS AURELIUS

I've alluded to this sentiment several times. When I read the thoughts Marcus Aurelius penned in *Meditations,* it was this quote that stood out to me the most. It is a privilege to be alive. Consider the thousands of people in our history who have died from war, plague, famine. What if Luigi had died in battle that day in Libya? What if Big D had followed his brothers to heaven as a baby or been killed during WWII?

Life is, indeed, a privilege and not one that should be taken lightly. Every morning when we awake, we have the opportunity to once again breathe the air, to think of a new idea, to enjoy a strong cup of coffee, to love our family and friends, to lay the foundations of a legacy. Life is a privilege, and my brand focuses on purveying products that help people enjoy those privileges.

Liberty Alliance is still going strong to this day, and along the way, I have learned something very important about myself. Politics and the business of politics are a means to an end. Yes, I am conserva-

127

tive, patriotic, religious, and a capitalist because I believe living with these ideologies and values yields peace, prosperity, and opportunity for all who are willing to reach out and work for them. As Henry Ford said, "Whether you think you can, or you think you can't, you're right."

When you are prosperous and at peace, you want to savor the fruits of your labor—and well you should, for you have earned the right to do so.

My trips to Italy solidified this mind-set. Italians enjoy dinners that last three hours and more. They savor some wine . . . and some more wine. There's always time to drop everything and spend time with family over a café or a shot of sambuca.

The hospitality for strangers I have witnessed in Italy is nothing short of astounding. Visiting Italy really began to demonstrate to me the vast importance of making the enjoyment of life's privileges part of your daily life.

Twice, I have had the opportunity to visit cousins descended from Luigi's second marriage. Without a moment's hesitation, they put aside their personal plans in order to meet me for dinner. I planned to simply slip away from the area, having said farewell the previous evening after much laughter and camaraderie over freshly made Neapolitan pizza and Italian beer.

"When are you leaving?" my cousin Pietro asked, always practicing his English. "We'll meet you for café and dolci tomorrow morning." And they did. One by one, nearly every family member joined us for a moment or two the next morning before proceeding on their busy work day.

Another example of hospitality that absolutely blew me away was when we visited the vineyard from which Vallorani Estates imports wine.

After our tour of the operations, we started to say our goodbyes and thank-yous. Rocco said, "Oh, but wait, we have a lunch prepared for you."

Rocco's entire family had never met us before that day, never talked to us, and yet they served us the most amazing multiple-course, homemade meal. They were not begrudging with their hospitality and, certainly, no expectations had been set that they would provide for us. There was not a hint of reluctance in their generosity.

This experience was one of the highlights of the trip, a refreshingly open and warm hospitality given freely to virtual strangers. All I could think while we were sitting at their table in their living room was how much I wanted to share this kind of experience with the world. Life is short. It's high time we started to enjoy it and the privileges it brings.

On a personal level, I have realized how quickly life passes us by. I am in my forties now, and I have lost my grandmother Edith and my grandfather Big D. My oldest baby girl is now married. The children still at home grow faster and faster each day, it seems. My businesses consume much of my time. When I'm not traveling to expand my brand or build relationships with clients and vendors, I am in meetings, answering the phone, and solving challenges continuously.

We can often become so involved in watching for wolves, eyeing wolves closing in, and escaping from wolves that we miss out on the opportunity to play the mandolin and enjoy the sounds of music wafting on the breeze.

I've always been very idealistic and built my businesses on sheer optimism, enthusiasm, idealism, opportunism—everything positive. Early on, I took people at face value and gave everyone the benefit of the doubt. But my naiveté and trusting nature sometimes allowed the wrong people to get too close.

If you become a successful entrepreneur, this may happen to you as well. There will be those people whom you bring in very close and who will turn on you—the wolves in sheep's clothing, if you will. They have been permitted in your inner circle but betray that trust, causing emotional or financial harm. They have been barred from my life entirely—gone. You can and should forgive, but you can't remain in a business or personal friendship with those who betray your trust.

Those decisions were difficult, and it has been painful to work through the havoc left in their wake, but each situation has certainly proved to be a valuable learning experience, and my team and I are stronger for having experienced the lesson. Though far from cynical, I'm much shrewder and sharper now, drawing on my inner Luigi to realize that not everyone has good intentions or blemish-free motives and to be cautious of those wolves in sheep's clothing.

As my businesses experienced explosive growth and those in my life saw me experience success, I began discovering who my true friends were. Some people were envious of me, and some celebrated with me. Eventually, I could count my closest friends on one hand. While success attracts success and thus successful people are attracted to other successful people, others are likely to resent your success. It is simply unavoidable.

Another thing I've learned in my forties is that I really know less now than I thought I did when I was younger. I'm less dogmatic than I was ten years ago. A few generations ago, people abstained from discussing religion and politics in polite company. Your personal beliefs were exactly that: personal. You lived your life the way you needed to live it and let everyone else do the same. It was a more tolerant and reasonable way to live, and increasingly, I find myself drawn to that philosophy.

Over the past two decades, I've met people with whom I would totally disagree, politically, even religiously, but they are people whose company is enjoyable. They are as interested in me as I am in them. I've realized we may not see eye to eye on a topic, but I like them, and I'll gladly share a drink with them and talk about what we have in common.

When a group of people gather in a room where no two might agree on political or religious platforms, I'll utilize my ability to get us all talking and having a good time anyway because, let's face it, there is a lot more to enjoy in life than just controversial topics!

As I get older, what is becoming increasingly attractive and appealing to me is getting together with others to enjoy the good things in life and sharing the music of the mandolin with the world around me rather than divisively arguing about religious or political beliefs.

A desire to share mandolin moments and encourage others to enjoy the privileges life provides is what prompted the creation of my Vallorani Estates brand. Not only am I personally enjoying every product we curate or create, but they're absolutely the finest products I can recommend. If I'm going to put my name on a product, it must not be mediocre or even good. It must be great.

I'd like to share stories of some of our products with you and explain how and why each of them was chosen to be part of Vallorani Estates.

Vallorani Cigars

One product that really resonates with me is my cigar line. My initial partiality for cigars may be related to the family story of Luigi and the scorpion. I'm always looking for products with that kind of personal feel attached to them. As an adult, I'd learned to enjoy a good cigar as one of life's great leisurely pleasures because you can't smoke a cigar in a hurry. It's the polar opposite of the high-speed living most of us do these days, and much more old world in the sense that the old world still knows how to pause and smell the roses. If you don't believe me, go to dinner at an Italian's home in Italy. You'll be at the table for hours, and you'll relish every moment.

It was on a hunting trip with my friend and business partner Doug Giles when I learned the true art of smoking and choosing a great cigar. It wasn't just about grabbing any cigar but selecting one that's of high quality and savoring it at the right time with the right drink. That time might be kicking off a hunting trip or celebrating the big kill. It wasn't just the cigar; it was the celebration it enhanced.

Doug loves to smoke cigars and knows the great ones from the good ones. It was on this hunting trip we took together that he suggested, "Hey, since we're successful website partners, why don't we start a cigar line? I've got a guy we can buy cigars from in Nicaragua. We can private label them." I said, "Why not? Let's do it."

We applied for our tobacco license. We got labels designed and printed. We imported a shipment of cigars, a highly rated producer of hand-wrapped cigars, and started selling Safari Cigars. We did that for a couple of years, very casually, more as a hobby than trying to make money at it. We reached the point where Doug's son-in-law wanted to buy me out. I agreed to it as long as I could continue to import the same cigars and sell them under my own label, Vallorani Cigars.

The Luigi and the Aurelius are fantastic cigars. Really, I have yet to smoke a better one, and everyone I've shared them with has found them nothing short of astounding. That's what makes it exciting for me to offer them to the public—because I know when people receive a Vallorani Estates product, they will not be disappointed. I would not sell a product I thought somebody would be disappointed with. I put my name, Luigi's name, on my products. You know they're good if I do that. I can't let down his legacy or my own.

Vallorani Coffee

Another product that resonates for me came to my attention by accident. One of my employees, Eric Rauch, had been roasting coffee at home and bringing it in to drink at the office. I could smell it down the hallway in my office. At that point I had a Keurig in my office, but I would tell my assistant, "I don't want it. Go get some of Eric's good coffee." Ten minutes later, I'd have a blissful cup of the best coffee I'd ever had. It smelled amazing. It tasted amazing. Soon I began to realize the coffee was so good that I no longer needed cream and sugar.

I told Eric, "Why don't you bring this in for the whole staff? You roast the coffee, I'll buy the beans." He said, "I'll need a bigger roaster to roast for the office." He was using a tiny countertop roaster.

We canceled our subscription to the crummy, stale, office-coffee delivery service, and Eric started bringing in the good stuff he was roasting from home on a bigger roaster we had bought. It wasn't long after that when I realized we could sell this coffee to the public. I hate hoarding life's privileges!

Again, we'd need a much bigger roaster if we wanted to sell coffee on that kind of scale. So we upgraded to a larger roaster . . . and today, due to demand, we use an even larger commercial roaster to double our output to one hundred pounds per day! We made the choice to provide the public with a full, sixteen-ounce bag of freshly roasted coffee beans instead of the industry-standard, twelve-ounce bag that starts as sixteen ounces and loses mass as it roasts.

Eric and his department came up with the name Thrasher Coffee because the brown thrasher is the Georgia state bird. Our Thrasher logo is very popular, and people love the brand, especially locally. Our online store offers autodeliveries to save time and money, or even a sampler of the variety of roasts and blends we carry. Customers might like espresso and decaf this month and a medium-dark blend next month. We thought over every detail to get it just right.

For everything I've ever enjoyed I've wondered how to make money by providing the same enjoyment to the public. So the segue into a coffee business didn't seem like such a stretch, though I had no real idea how to successfully sell a boutique food product over the Internet.

Mass-market consumers are often looking for cheap prices, particularly if they cannot taste the quality before purchasing. Unlike a bumper sticker that is what it is, coffee can be a stale, big-box-brand canister dug out of the back of a pantry, or it can be a craft coffee, freshly roasted in small batches to provide a gourmet experience.

It became quickly apparent that I was going to experience a challenge with this business because I was trying to mass-market gourmet coffee over the Internet, and until they could figure out the teleporter, I couldn't give people a sample before they committed to the value.

That's when, out of the blue, Seth Gragg contacted us and gave us his resume—sales experience and management experience. Yet he's the most down-to-earth guy you could imagine. He's not a slick salesman. He's just a real authentic human being who loves his coffee. He truly believes in the product. He is a rock star and owns his role completely. Once we brought him aboard, the business doubled its revenue.

Since Eric, who helped get Thrasher Coffee off the ground, moved on to another position, Seth has been a one-man band determining the source, roasting the beans, and making local sales. People buy locally because of Seth's presentations at events and businesses. He also has been instrumental in working with Liz and me to establish client relationships in order to customize private-label coffee brands that are sourced by Thrasher Coffee.

The Thrasher brand has become popular, but I wanted to create a luxury, Italian-themed brand for Vallorani Estates, so I also created my own coffee line: Vallorani Coffee. We currently offer an Italian roast called Buon Giorno, which has been a top-selling favorite with it's chocolaty notes that also hint of blueberries. We also created a high-caffeine blend as our alternative to Death Wish Coffee, named Elysium. Elysium is the paradise of the blessed, according to classic Greco-Roman mythology. Why wish for death when you can experience Elysium?

Seth has been one of the best hiring decisions I've ever made. He's got us into a plethora of local shops and cafes and even local grocery stores. Additional large grocery store opportunities are lining up currently.

My eldest daughter, Bethany, is our director of marketing. Thanks to her efforts in social media and email marketing, she assisted Seth in quadrupling sales in a single year. A big inspiration for me has been recalling the pleasure my grandfather Big D took in his cups of strong coffee. The smell of freshly roasted Vallorani Coffee brings that memory back every day.

One of our repeated compliments has been from the light-and-sweet coffee drinkers who agree with me that they don't need sweetener anymore because our coffee tastes so good.

Have you ever considered that coffee can have tasting notes similar to that of wine? I hadn't until I experienced the flavors of an amazingly good, freshly roasted coffee that had my taste buds exploding over hints of toasted marshmallows or blueberries and dark chocolate.

Vallorani Wine

Quality is what sets my products apart, and that goes for the wine I love to drink as well. There was a time when I could drink liquor all night long. The first thing I'd do when I got home was pour some vodka on the rocks to de-stress from the busy workday, and I would de-stress well into the evening.

In 2016 I made the decision to stop drinking this way for health reasons. I want to be around to enjoy my grandchildren, and possibly, my great-grandchildren. If my liver is shot, I won't get to experience that privilege.

Now, my alcohol consumption is much more deliberate and thoughtful and reserved for special occasions. I select my drink thoughtfully. I savor it. It's a special enjoyment. It's so much more enjoyable than feeling I have to drink every night to drown my stress.

When you're drinking that way, you honestly don't even taste it any more.

When you stop being able to taste a food or beverage and it has become something you require to survive, whether it's tobacco or alcohol or anything else, I think you're missing out on the real benefit of that privilege. You're potentially endangering your health if it gets to that level. Moderation is the key.

Of course, you're free to live your life however you want, but I'd had enough of this modern grab-and-go lifestyle. I now seek to enjoy mandolin moments on a more contemplative level and encourage others to do so as well.

I started growing grapes in 2012 as a result of talking with my grandfather about how he and Luigi used to make wine together. In 2011 when my brother, father, grandfather, and I made our special trip to Italy, it was grape harvest time. We were driving back to the hotel after having eaten at Big D's favorite restaurant outside of Offida, Italy, when he said, "Raymond, pull over to the side of the road. Brandon, get me some of those grapes," and he pointed to a vineyard by the roadside.

I wasn't sure if I was allowed, but my father said, "When Big D speaks, listen." What could I say? "And pick some olives too," Big D continued. So we pulled over, jumped out of the car, and grabbed a small handful of grapes and some olives. Big D didn't want to eat the olives really, just look at them. Those grapes were delicious.

He started telling me all about how he and his dad, Luigi, used to make wine. He even shared a recipe—very basic—and the process they went through. It wasn't enough to really get started on, but it was enough to inspire me to go home and plant grapevines.

At the time, I only had about three acres, but my landscaper, Randal, and I brought two-year-old vines from a winery in California and planted French and Italian wine grapes: cabernet, chardonnay, merlot, pinot grigio, pinot noir, and sangiovese. Eric, who helped start Thrasher Coffee, was extremely interested in wine, so he helped me make our first twenty bottles of wine from the small batch of grapes we gained from our first harvest in 2013.

At this point, wine making was an experiment, purely a hobby, just rolling the dice and playing around. It was a nod to Luigi and Big D more than anything. I wasn't actually planning on making a business with wine.

Then, one day, Eric casually mentioned to me, "Brandon, I was doing some research and I found out there's a vineyard in Italy with your last name, Vigneti Vallorani." I checked, and it turned out they were located near Offida, Italy, where my grandfather had spent most of his childhood and where Luigi was from originally.

Needless to say, I was astonished and intrigued. We found the vineyard on Facebook and got in touch with Rocco, the founder. This wine is very popular in Italy, and we couldn't wait to try it.

Shortly thereafter, Liz came into my office for a signature. She had filled out all the paperwork to apply for a permit to import wine into the US. This is one example of the steps taken by many of my employees to expand our arena of influence. As I mentioned earlier, they climb a hill because they are inspired to carry out my vision.

In 2015 we imported our first shipment of Vigneti Vallorani wine. The Italian company also grows olives and manufactures olive oil, which we're also now importing. It is absolutely the best olive oil I've ever tasted. You could almost make popsicles from it!

In the Marche region of Italy, Rocco founded the business from the grapevines his grandfather had planted years before. As the industrial age took over that region back in the early 1900s, landowners were selling off their vineyards and their land to seek higher profits in factories. The Italian government made a law that they must give first right of sale to those who had been working that land.

Livio Vallorani, Rocco's grandfather, had been working this land, and he and a friend determined to purchase a small chunk of it. A couple of generations later, Rocco took it from a farm making wine for the family to a much bigger enterprise. Vigneti Vallorani currently produces twenty thousand bottles annually, which are enjoyed nationally in Italy and are now available in the US through Vallorani Estates.

Rocco, in his thirties, not only went to school to study viticulture but also worked with internationally recognized vineyards in New Zealand and in Oregon. He wrote a thesis on various techniques and, essentially, has the equivalent of a master's degree in viticulture. Not only is he a skilled vintner but he also has proved to be a brilliant marketer and a like-minded compatriot.

The business is run completely by him, his younger brother, and his dad. They recruit friends to pick grapes for the annual harvest. Following Rocco's developmental ideas, they'll be increasing their bottling output to between thirty-five and forty thousand annually within the next year or two due to vineyard expansion. As I am doing, Rocco's carrying his family legacy forward and has turned it into a viable and growing business.

Liz, Tracey, and I went to meet Rocco face to face to see where and how we could expand our globally connected partnership to provide the privileges of life to the world. Until then, I hadn't really understood how Rocco operated or the synergies between our businesses.

Considering the output and the highly rated quality of the wine, I expected a massive business with dozens of workers scurrying around in big offices.

When we arrived, we found a beautiful yet modest home, nestled in the hillside overlooking my ancestor's Apennine mountains. We were greeted by two tail-wagging dogs, happy to see visitors. Rocco appeared from around the side of the house, welcoming us to his place in exceptional English.

We walked nearly every inch of the property as he explained which grapes were planted on which sides of the hills and pointed out vines his grandfather had planted sixty-five years earlier. I took lots of photographs of how everything operated, wishing to mirror it back home in my own small vineyard. Rocco's knowledge is impressive. What an amazing operation is tucked away in those hills!

Each wine has a name and a story. But what really surprised and touched us was that while we were enjoying this fabulous tour of the vineyard and its operations, his mother and father had been preparing an amazing—and massive—lunch for us. Neither of them spoke a word of English, but the warm hospitality with which they came out to meet us and bring us to the table was genuine: "Sit! Mangia! [Eat!]"

They had prepared carbonara . . . and roasted chicken . . . and salad . . . and killer, fried, stuffed olives—all preceded by antipasto of fresh mozzarella, prosciutto, salami, and mortadella. Each course was accompanied by vineyard wine pairings. As we sat back to loosen our belts, fruit and pastries and, of course, café and sambuca were presented.

Their warmth and hospitality was nothing short of inspiring. I knew then that I wanted to create this same kind of "Come in, come in, eat, enjoy!" hospitality that our Italian counterparts offered to us so freely back here in the US.

After dinner, we started talking through our family trees because having the same last name and origins in the same town of Italy seems to guarantee a connection. Rocco translated for his parents, and they nodded and agreed in Italian. We are still working with an ancestry research firm to help us make the connection between Rocco's grandfather Livio and my great-grandfather Luigi.

Then I had the privilege of offering a Vallorani cigar to Rocco's father, Giancarlo. He lit up immediately and enjoyed it right there in the house with a huge smile on his face. I've got pictures of Giancarlo and Rocco and Rocco's brother Stefano smoking Vallorani Estate's Luigi cigars.

Looking back, it was a most memorable moment as I marveled that this was a reuniting of the Vallorani family. Smoking Luigi cigars in Luigi's stomping grounds with these great partners and getting to share the enjoyment of life's privileges together was an amazing and life-changing occasion.

One of the things I particularly like about Vigneti Vallorani's operation is how eco-friendly and thoughtful the owners are about how they grow grapes and use energy. They only grow grapes indigenous to that region, and they use traditional wine-making techniques. They don't use pesticides, preferring instead to adhere to the pest prevention provided naturally by the ecosystem. For example, there are bugs whose young, when hatched, will cause rot inside the grape clusters. Letting grass grow close to the vines allows spiders to eat these egg-laying bugs and also enhances the flavor of the grapes as they fight with the grass for the earth's nutrients.

Vigneti Vallorani also produces 80 percent of its energy through solar power and natural-cooling methods. Rocco

Vallorani is an astute man with visionary passion to create a world-renowned and eco-friendly winery, and we are honored to be a US partner with our Italian counterpart.

I really like that model of sustainability and conscious environmental friendliness. A lot of people imagine that capitalists will abuse the earth just to make money, but in fact, I take the job of looking after the planet we've been given very seriously.

Back home in Georgia I expanded, buying more land and planting two hundred additional vines of almost-exclusively Italian grapes. Sangiovese grapevines are grown on about a third of our vineyard now. I'm hoping 2017 will be a good harvest year.

As I try to establish my American version of the Vallorani vineyard, we continue to work with Rocco to provide the US public with an established, award-winning collection of wines that already bears my last name on the labels.

Initially, we'll be selling four of their wines: Zaccari is a white wine and represents the kind of family nickname found in an area populated by many with the same last name. The second wine, Avora, is one of the crispest, freshest, and most delicious white wines I've ever enjoyed. It is named for the cool exposure from the Adriatic Sea breeze that kisses the grapes growing on the north/northeast-facing hillside. Koné, a word in the local dialect that means "something of great value," is a premium red wine. My personal favorite is the red wine named Polisia, which is the name of a local legend involving a Roman governor's daughter, back when the Christians were being persecuted by the Roman Empire.

Polisia was converted by a Catholic monk and baptized into the Christian faith. Her father was livid when he learned of it and went after her, intending to kill her for abandoning his pagan tradition.

To escape him, Polisia ran up the mountain nearby, which is called Monte Ascensione, and, they say, fairies protected her from her father's wrath and helped her hide on the mountain, where she now watches over the valley to protect it. Apparently, there was a large earthquake in the area some time ago, and, according to legend, the area was completely untouched due to the protection of its patron saint, Polisia.

We were on our way out the door, stuffed with the wine and food Rocco and his family had so generously provided when we were asked if we had seen the nearby town, Ascoli Piceno. Upon learning we had not, Rocco exclaimed without hesitation, "I'll take you!"

A short distance away we were enraptured by this small city, which oozes inspiration and charm like nothing else witnessed. Over three hundred churches dot the narrow streets that wind around buildings standing on the ruins of old Roman roads. An ancient Roman bridge spans the river, and the piazza in the center of the town is now only open to foot traffic to preserve the history and nostalgia.

Clock towers and cobblestones, reverent churches untouched by tourism, street market vendors purveying goods ranging from fried olives to fish to flowers, a coffee café unchanged for one hundred years—what a remarkable moment in time, this Italy not long separated from the era of my ancestors.

This part of Italy was really a revelation to me. I remember walking up those steep hills and seeing the Apennine Mountains in the background, knowing that the foothills of those mountains were where my grandmother Italia "Edith" DeDonato and my uncle

143

Dom, "the fox of industrial wizardry," came from. I could actually see her village in the far distance from the hilltop of the vineyard as Rocco pointed it out to me. All day, the story of the wolves and the mandolin resonated in my mind as I walked in the shadow of the mountains where that legendary story was formed.

As we drove through those cold, stark, but stunning Apennine Mountains on our way back to Rome, we passed through a ten-kilometer tunnel built in the 1980s to allow passage across those wolf-inhabited mountains. It was a bright, sunny day when we entered the tunnel, but dark clouds and falling snow greeted us on the other side. It's a stunning part of the world, still wild and treacherous through all it's beauty.

When did I realize I'd shifted my life's mission from selling products to promoting a lifestyle? It first began with the stories of Luigi told by my grandpa Big D. It evolved with visits to Italy and really hit home when my staff handed me the first bottle of Vallorani wine and I saw my name on the label from that 2013 harvest. I think, at that moment, I realized I wanted to turn this legacy of the Vallorani name into a brand others could enjoy along with me.

It hit home again when I was at the West Virginia Italian Heritage Festival in 2015, showcasing my coffee and cigars, and I tied it together with a whole new line and philosophy. We had a picture of Luigi, we were telling stories about Luigi, and we were pushing the name of Vallorani because that name is known and recognizable, and I asked myself why we weren't doing this all the time, everywhere.

The Vallorani name as a brand makes perfect sense. People work so hard to create marketing angles and stories around their brands, and here I was, with a whole book's worth of stories to tell about my family heritage that tied back to the beginning in Italy.

It seems to be a daunting journey ahead right now as most of our projects are in the starting phase, but my business partner Liz continually states with confidence that the Vallorani brand can and will be as well-known as the name Armani one day.

I would like to think that Luigi is beaming with pride at the legacy he has left. I know that Big D is, because he was very proud of our products. He even drank a bottle of Vallorani wine from that 2013 harvest! Yes, he said, "It's pretty good!"

We've made a lot of progress. Since 2015, Vallorani Estates has been establishing a name at numerous, local, independent shops and community events and is partnering with Kennesaw State University's athletic department. We got in on the ground floor by providing our Vallorani wines and Vallorani coffees at their hospitality suites and fan zones at football and basketball games.

Not far from Kennesaw State University is one of our biggest and most ambitious dreams to date: the Villa Vallorani.

Villa Vallorani

I have always dreamed of creating an "eat-work-enjoy" kind of multi-use facility where people can experience the Vallorani Estates line of products in an inviting and unique location. Recently, a new retail development opened in downtown Kennesaw, and we looked into renting space there. However, the amount of red tape the lawyers and landlords were imposing on us for a space that wasn't even optimal made us decide against it. We would have invested hundreds of thousands of dollars building out a space that wasn't, ultimately, our own.

Meanwhile, in Kennesaw's historic district, a Victorian manor was slipping into the overgrowth on the corner of Main Street. The building had formerly operated as a B&B and event venue but had been empty and abandoned for several years, as the owners were entangled in divorce proceedings.

Our realtor connected us with the broker, and upon touring it, we found it to be structurally sound. It was just buried in junk and trash, begging to shine as a destination once more. The expansive mansion was listed for a fraction of its value, but we found that it was also only weeks away from foreclosure and, as a consequence, a bidding war on the courthouse steps.

Due to some red flags with the title, our bank was unable to fund a mortgage, and there was no way the property would still be available when the business loan came through for us after a lengthy financial investigation in the underwriting process.

Just as I had persisted in taking my trip to Cancun, I wasn't going to let the "no" wolves keep me from seizing this opportunity to expand the Vallorani legacy in our local area!

We went into overdrive. The broker went to bat for us, and the title issues were cleared up. I had about half of the money in savings, and we borrowed the rest from friends and family. Every wolf that circled around us was fended off, allowing me to close on the property just a few days before foreclosure proceedings—outright, with cash. That was quite a day!

We went back to the bank and obtained the loan we needed to renovate the place. Tony, the handyman I have worked with for years, helped us clean up the massive amount of junk, and what a difference that made!

Now we are in the process of completing the necessary renovations with our general contractor, Vito, who just happens to be an Italian too. Villa Vallorani will be a showcase for the Vallorani Estates brand and provide a much-needed local gathering spot to encourage the enjoyment of the privileges of life in the metro-Atlanta area.

I love history, and I love creating new opportunities, so for me, restoring this magnificent building is the perfect marriage of both pursuits: a nod to the past while also looking forward to the future. One of our goals is to share our celebration of Italian heritage and quality with a community that is currently lacking Italian cultural influences.

Italians have contributed so much to American culture—science, engineering, history—and so much of what has been accomplished has been ignored or forgotten. I'd like to change that.

Villa Vallorani is in the perfect location, an up-and-coming hot spot for our local community of college students, young professionals, and growing families. Plus, it creates several viable revenue streams by allowing us to have a coffee shop, a small-plates wine bar and café, and a venue for hosting special occasions such as business events and family gatherings.

Most importantly, it is monumental for me to put the name Vallorani on a shingle in our area and provide the community with Vallorani quality goods that share the privileges of life with others around me.

Villa Vallorani actually sits on the highest point in Kennesaw, overlooking Kennesaw Mountain, just below the spot my father and I optimistically claimed as a future birthplace of the Vallorani legacy in Georgia.

At Villa Vallorani, I don't care what you believe or think about religion or politics. I don't care who got your vote in the election. Come experience Villa Vallorani and enjoy life's privileges. I want you to walk out and say, "I just experienced the Vallorani lifestyle. I just experienced the enjoyment of life. I just enjoyed the music of the mandolin. I can face the wolves again."

In the political business I've established, I've effectively cut myself off from half the United States by standing with one political party against another. Don't get me wrong. I am still a conservative, but I am less concerned with fighting political foes these days and more interested in finding great things and great experiences friends can unite over: an amazing glass of Vallorani wine, a great cup of Vallorani coffee, the aroma of a fantastic Vallorani cigar. These mandolin moments are what make fighting off the wolves of life worthwhile.

Now, that doesn't mean that my personal beliefs have changed. It's simply that I would rather talk politics over a good cigar in a friendly manner than with a drive-by assault by bumper sticker. Looking back, though, I can see this evolving mentality has been a trend in my business career. Every vine I've grabbed has, effectively, broadened my market a little bit to reach more people. I'm not content to stick to a niche, and I don't want to be forced into a box.

What's driving this change? I'd say it's a combination of growing up, having some tough experiences, and really getting in touch with who I am and what *really* matters to me. I've always enjoyed the good life. I respect and embrace quality. I learned early on that I can't go cheap.

Whenever I try to cut corners to be cheap it's backfired in my face. If I try to buy something second-rate to save a buck, it invariably ends up costing me many times more than it would have cost if I'd chosen the better quality in the first place, even before I factor in the wear and tear of aggravation. One cup of good coffee is worth two cups of terrible coffee.

I also hate to hoard. When I find something good, I can't wait to share it with others. Being able to help others experience the privileges of life keeps me going in a world rife with wolves.

Perhaps I have reached the halftime of my life. I've spent the first half of my life learning who I am and what I want to do with my life. Now I'm reflecting. I'm writing this book. I'm thinking over where I've been and where I want to go. The products that I'm creating carry my family name, and I'm curating other products that my family would also be proud to share.

To me, Vallorani Estates brings everything back, full circle, to the beginning of this book and our family legend. Life brings many wolves across our path. We can challenge them head-on to a fight and possibly lose or, at best, come out badly scarred. We can climb a tree and hide out, fearful for our lives, and hold out until we're hungry and sore from clinging to the branch just out of reach of their ever-snapping jaws. Or we can rest in the crook of the tree and play the mandolin and enjoy the star-lit night and the sounds of a sweet melody, and we can soothe those wolves so they leave us alone.

At the time I was experimenting with these products, I didn't realize they were converging into a family brand. I jumped into the coffee business because I enjoyed better coffee than what we were being sold and thought others should experience it with me. I enjoyed better cigars than those I'd had on the golf course and wanted to share them.

In traveling around the world, eating at Michelin-rated restaurants, and being presented with wine options by a world-class sommelier, you start realizing that just as spending money on good clothes can make you feel better about yourself, a better cigar, a better cup of coffee, or a better wine will, sometimes, help you live a better life. Yes, you get what you pay for. Why go cheap and enjoy it half as much? Why not fully embrace the enjoyment of life's privileges?

When I look back at the moment when my dad and I stood on Kennesaw Mountain and admired the vast terrain of Cobb and Paulding counties in Georgia, I think, *Wow. That was just twelve years ago, and look how far we've come.* I own so much property here now. I own many successful businesses. Now I've bought one of the most historic and majestic properties, on the highest point in Kennesaw, to turn into a showcase for our products and a tribute to our family history.

Continuing a legacy for—and with—my family is paramount. Recently, I was thrilled to partner with my dad, my sister, Karissa, and her husband, Jared, on a new venture together. My cousin, Lisa, and her husband, Chris, partner with me in a different project. It's not just about creating MY name as a brand but continuing the Vallorani legacy as a whole family. I want my kids to love working in our business, I want our grandkids to be proud to carry on the legacy. Not only do I want to preserve our family history, I also want to share the mandolin moments that I am getting to experience. I'm not a loner, so it gives me a lot of joy to share the privileges of life with others. And it's more fun to enjoy together than it is to keep it all to myself!

Preserve family history, create a legacy, and share the rewards—those are my new life goals. Once Villa Vallorani is open and my brands are established and people are coming to see the family legacy, I believe it will open up all kinds of new doors and take us to the next step. As I said earlier, success breeds success. People will respond; the word will spread.

We're not finished adding products to my line. There is a plethora of food products, liquor products, flavored salts, clothing, accessories, and all kinds of things from the area my ancestors came from in Italy, just waiting to be discovered and enjoyed.

Our most recent product-acquisition plans are to import from the Valdobbiadene region a prosecco not yet found in the US. We even envision hosting tours to the beautiful countryside found at my ancestor's homesteads, where you can drink wine on a balcony overlooking vineyards and villages untouched by time and stress!

There's also something called the pepperoni roll, local to where I came from in the Italian American settlements of western Pennsylvania and West Virginia. Very basic—it's just pepperoni baked into dough, sometimes joined by mozzarella. Simple, and simply delicious, it was the kind of lunch an Italian immigrant could carry down into the mines because it wouldn't spoil during a long day. In every gas station, and in every grocery store, you can buy pepperoni rolls. My mom made me pepperoni rolls to take to school. I just assumed that everybody enjoyed pepperoni rolls, until I left West Virginia and discovered nobody anywhere else had heard of this tasty delight.

That's why I am going to bring pepperoni rolls made in Clarksburg, which are some of my favorites, to Villa Vallorani and introduce Georgians to the pepperoni roll. I'd love that to be part of my legacy—to spread this enjoyment outside the West Virginia area.

That's my philosophy now, so you'll find Vallorani coffee, cigars, and wine in my home, in my Christmas gifts, and in the homes of my family and friends. I am proud to carry on the legend and legacy of Luigi Vallorani, of Eugene Vallorani, of my uncle Gene, and my dad. I hope to give my children that same pride in their last name, and their children after them.

Marcus Aurelius's words in the quote at the beginning of this chapter remind me to always be grateful for the privilege of life. I've enjoyed, and continue to enjoy, success in business and personal life, and now, with my Vallorani Estates line, I'm selling things that I personally use and believe in. To me, much of life and success is marketing, and marketing yourself is part of that, especially when your name is on the products you're selling.

That's why I'm more conscious than ever that the quality of my products has to be top-notch and that who I am will have an impact on whom I attract with my brands, in my businesses, and among my inner circle.

I've done some thinking about how that works, based on my own experiences, and I'd like to offer some suggestions.

Life is marketing. When people first see you, you have about seven seconds to make a good—or bad—impression. If you carry yourself well, if you're dressed nicely and look healthy, if you can speak articulately, if you're genuinely interested in other people, it makes a great first impression. If you shake their hands, look them in the eye, and remember their name, they'll remember that you made them feel they mattered to you.

Do this enough times, and you create an aura about yourself. You attract people who'll want to be part of your inner circle, and they will believe in your brand and, in turn, you can help them realize their own dreams.

I think back to how I felt as a kid, seeing my uncle Gene's lifestyle—the gracious home, the pool, the steaks, and his cigars—remembering how much I wanted all that even as a kid and how it kick-started my ambitions. My goal is to provide that kind of example for my kids and their friends, and everyone who comes in contact with the Vallorani Estates brand.

Be what you want to attract. The way that you carry yourself, the clothes that you choose to wear, the words that you say, the things you talk about, the car you drive and how well it's cared for, the posts that you share on Facebook—all of these things are important to your overall brand. Let's talk about why.

Frequently, I see people post on Facebook, complaining about how bad their day was or how this person hurt them and so forth. What they're asking for is sympathy: "Let me get as much sympathy as I can get from others. Tell me how bad I have it. Poor me." I don't do that, and I don't enable those who do. Seek to only post positive things about others and the highlights of your own day. Life can be good, and that's what we should want to project and, in turn, attract. Focus on the mandolin, not the wolves.

Polish your elevator pitch because you never know when you'll need it. I recently met a man who's done something very successfully. Now he is trying to make a living by letting other people use his idea. He spent thirty minutes hemming and hawing as he tried to explain what it is he does and what value he provides. This is not a great way to inspire confidence. If you make a pitch like that, you're telling me you don't know exactly what you do, and even if you do know, why should I choose you over the next vendor who has the ability to describe to me the specific value he or she offers?

Why should I listen? Why do you provide greater value than the next person? You need to be articulate enough to carry on a conversation, to present what it is you do, how you do it, and why you do it if you want to inspire confidence in your ability.

What I Know to Be True

My family and my family name are my most valuable possessions. That's why I'd never put the Vallorani name on any product I don't use and enjoy myself.

At this stage in my life and adventures, I want to share the privileges of life with others, to remind them that life is for enjoying, and every moment we have is a gift. Watch the sun rise, and celebrate the new day with a great cup of coffee. Enjoy a relaxing interlude with a great cigar, or better yet, with a good friend and two cigars and a great bottle of wine.

Take the time to listen to the music of the mandolin because even the most beautiful song can't last forever. Savor the privileges of life, and share them with those around you.

"If wisdom were offered me on the one condition that I should keep it shut away and not divulge it to anyone, I should reject it. There is no enjoying the possession of anything valuable unless one has someone to share it with."—Seneca

IN CLOSING . . .

This book began with my family's story of the wolves and the mandolin. Life is very busy and full of wolves. Every day there is something: A child gets hurt and ends up in the emergency room. An employee struggles to deliver satisfactory results. A boss may be chomping at your heels. The wolves seem to circle around, doing their best to keep you from enjoying the small moments that make it all worthwhile.

Thinking back now about all the wolves my family encountered, and those I have encountered in my life, it's nothing short of a miracle that I can now enjoy the music of the mandolin over the howls of those wolves.

I know I'm not alone.

There are a lot of people like me out there, meeting for coffee, talking over wine, posting on social media about the good things in life. They're posting photos of their families, of great meals or trips they've enjoyed, sharing the highlights of their lives. The moments that echo the sweet strain of the mandolin keep the wolves of life from taking over and destroying us.

Life is short and full of many wolves, so let's find the moments to make it as sweet as possible. There's an old Italian proverb: "If you cannot live longer, live deeper."

I would like to encourage others to live more deeply by finding the good in life. Don't let the pack of wolves bring you down. Despite the fact that they're at the bottom of the tree and snarling at your feet, you can still find the time to enjoy life's privileges and experience happiness wherever you are.

As Marcus Aurelius pointed out nearly two thousand years ago, the happiness of your life depends upon the quality of your thoughts, and that hasn't changed.

I've learned that it doesn't just happen. You have to make an effort to take the time to enjoy life's small, sweet pleasures, and I like to help others find them. Take the time to savor life's privileges.

It's a privilege to pause to enjoy a great cup of high-quality, freshly roasted coffee and not just knock back a caffeine shot of low-grade, stale grinds as you rush to work. It's a privilege to open a special bottle of wine, crafted with care and with its own history and story to tell, and share it with family and friends. It's a privilege to smoke a great cigar, whether it's to celebrate a highlight moment or just to pause and contemplate your good fortune.

The good things take time. For instance, we encourage people to use a French press to make our coffee. It takes a little more time, yes, but it releases the flavor much more fully, and the liturgy of grinding freshly roasted coffee beans and steeping them before pressing and pouring the coffee creates an overarching sense of calm and sensory enjoyment too.

When you actually make the commitment to sit down and experience our products, you're reaching for that mandolin. Yes, the wolves might be down there in the form of bills piling up in the mailbox, the boss demanding your full attention, or the troubles your kids might be facing in school.

Nobody's life is without some turmoil or complications. But you can choose to pause, refocus, and enjoy the music of the mandolin. You can make music, and you can share it with others just as I have been able to through Vallorani Estates.

I'd love to hear from you. If you'd like to know more about my products and the lifestyle they celebrate, visit me at **brandonvallorani. com**. I'd be thrilled to introduce you to the privileges life has brought me and hear how you are enjoying them too.

Follow the Vallorani Estates brand and join Vita Vallorani at www.ValloraniEstates.com.

Brandon Vallorani is available for publicity and media inquiries, as well as in-person business and marketing consulting. You may contact us for scheduling through ValloraniEstates.com.

PHOTOS

Domenico Vallorani, father of Luigi Vallorani.

Luigi as a young man.

Maria and Luigi on their wedding day.

Maria holding baby Eugene.

Luigi walking two of his daughters down the aisle in Venice, Italy.

Luigi as an older man.

Luigi standing with his second wife and daughters outside of his Offida home.

Brandon standing in front of Luigi's Offida home (2016).

Eugene's passport from Rome's US Embassy.

Eugene (Big D) serving in the Pacific during WWII.

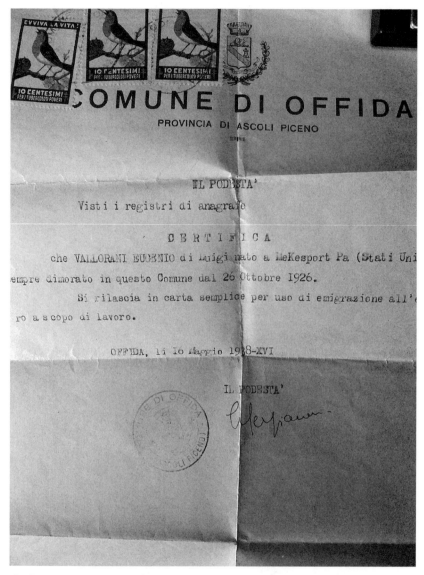

The letter stating Eugene Vallorani was a United States citizen, having been born in PA.

Eugene while working at Westinghouse.

Certificate of Recognition for Eugene's part in assisting with the Three Mile Island incident.

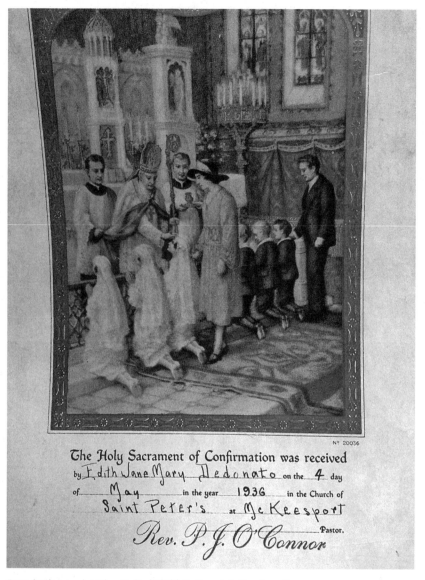

The Holy Sacrament of Confirmation was received by Edith Jane Mary DeDonato on the 4 day of May in the year 1936 in the Church of Saint Peter's at McKeesport

Rev. P. J. O'Connor Pastor.

Nº 20036

Brandon's grandmother Italia (Edith) DeDonato's Confirmation.

Brandon's cousin Lisa, Aunt Trina, cousin Melissa, Uncle Gene, Grandmother Edith, Brandon, and his father, Ray, at historic Kennywood Park in Pittsburgh, Pennsylvania.

Brandon and his mother, Linda.

Brandon, a true child of the '70s, always possessed a big imagination.

Big D and Edith dancing at a family wedding.

Brandon with his father Ray and grandfather Big D outside of Big D's home in McKeesport, PA.

171

Brandon with his maternal grandparents, Margaret and Hartley Burgreen.

Brandon with his family at Big D's 90th birthday celebration (2013).

Brandon and his great aunt Antonietta at Luigi's grave in 2016.

Brandon standing in the Piazza Valorani in Offida, Italy (2016).

173

L-R: Cousin Donatella's husband Piero, cousin Donatella, cousin Paula, Brandon, cousin Pietro, Pietro's son Leonardo, Pietro's son Francesco in Offida, Italy (2016).

Dinner with family...and more family . . . and friends! The more the merrier in Italy! (2016)

Brandon with his trophy whitetail. This 160 class buck was taken in Texas in November 2016 with a 30.06.

Brandon with his Père David's deer taken in Florida in 2013.

Brandon and his boys with an Axis buck that he shot at 350 yards in the Texas hill country in April 2015.

Brandon and the stabbed hog from chapter eight.

Brandon with his seven children (2016).

(L-R) Liz, Rocco, Brandon (and Argo) at Vigneti Vallorani (2016).

Brandon walking his daughter Bethany down the aisle (2016).

Brandon with his dogs Hank and Cassia—they're part of the family, too!